Scouting and Patrolling

Scouting *and* Patrolling

Waldron

Scouting *and* Patrolling

By

Captain William H. Waldron
29th U. S. Infantry

DISTINGUISHED GRADUATE INFANTRY AND
CAVALRY SCHOOL, 1905
GRADUATE ARMY STAFF COLLEGE, 1906
GRADUATE ARMY WAR COLLEGE, 1911
ASSISTANT DIRECTOR ARMY WAR
COLLEGE COURSE, 1911-12

Washington:
The United States Infantry Association
1916

Copyright, 1916, by
U. S. Infantry Association

NATIONAL CAPITAL PRESS, INC., WASHINGTON, D. C.

CONTENTS

INTRODUCTION

This little book has been prepared with the idea of placing before the regular soldier and the citizen soldier in readable form and in its logical sequence the information that may be of assistance in preparing him for the duties that may fall to his lot in time of war.

From a perusal of its pages, it will be noted that the first six chapters are devoted to the subjects that affect the training and methods of the individual scout. The seventh takes up the operations of a detachment of scouts called a patrol, and the remainder of the volume is designed to supply a text book covering the military subjects he will need to study to perfect himself as a scout. It has been the endeavor to deal with these latter in a purely elementary manner that any soldier or citizen should be able to understand.

If the book helps him over some of the rough places and increases his store of information on the subject it will have accomplished its purpose.

THE AUTHOR.

CHAPTER I

Importance of Information

The possession of accurate information about the enemy is one of the most important elements of success in war. It is the indispensable basis of all military plans, and nothing but faulty dispositions can be expected if it is lacking. Its acquisition is one of the most difficult tasks of the commander in the field. The numbers, the dispositions, and the movements of the opposing forces are veiled in an obscurity which has been aptly termed the "fog of war," an obscurity which all commanders will endeavor by every artifice to deepen.

The commander without information of his opponent is like a man blindfolded. He knows neither where to strike nor from what quarter to expect attack. He is unable to make plans for himself or to guard against those of the enemy. His tactical skill will avail him nothing, and the valor, skill and endurance of his troops will be wasted in vain attempts, unproductive of decisive results.

As soon as armies take the field, the pursuit of information on the one hand and the denying of it to the enemy on the other immediately become the serious, if not the paramount, considerations in the mind of the commander. Unless he can pierce the curtain of fog that surrounds his enemy while at the same time deepening that which surrounds his own troops, he will be unable to devise a scheme to compass his adversary's overthrow or to insure his own safety.

The comparative value of information as to the enemy's movements acquired by opposing forces is the determining factor between victory and defeat when opposing armies are equal in strength and equally well led. A weaker army acting on good information, should inevitably overcome a somewhat stronger army less well served in its intelligence.

Search military history, and it will be found that there has hardly been a great battle chronicled therein, the results of which have not been dependent upon the value of previous reconnaissance. Either the winners have won through knowing all about the numbers and dispositions of their opponents and have been able to direct their operations so as to insure success, or the loser has lost through his ignorance of these same elements.

The military commander that blunders into action without having first had a reconnaissance made to determine the enemy's strength and dispositions is doomed to defeat if not to disaster.

Aerial Reconnaissance Aeroplanes and airships have considerably enlarged the possibilities of reconnaissance, and there is no doubt but that they will be extensively employed in the wars of the future. Their operations are, however, subject to certain very definite limitations. In fogs, storms, or darkness, aerial observers find it most difficult to obtain definite information. The armament that has been developed for use against air-craft keeps them at great heights, which prevents detailed tactical reconnaissance. To this is added the development of the art of concealing troops and materiel to such an extent as to make them invisible to the air scouts. In view of these factors, aerial reconnaissance will be valuable in procuring strategic information involving large bodies of troops but can not, in its present state of advancement, replace the methods hitherto employed for gaining that detailed information of the enemy upon which tactical decisions may be based.

In the subject of tactics, we have to deal solely with military reconnaissance in contradistinction to topographical reconnaissance. Topography is a separate branch of military art and may be mastered by practice after gaining a theoretical knowledge from any one of the several excellent text books on the subject.

In war, the action of the most insignificant subordinate may turn the issue of a campaign. A battle may be won by the gallantry of a corporal who rallies a handful of men. The fate of empires may hang on the drowsiness of a sentry on outpost or the shaken nerves of a soldier ripe for panic. But of all the subordinates, it is the scout upon whose success or failure great issues are most likely to depend. The pursuit of information is so uncertain, so full of chances, that it may well be possible for a couple of scouts or a patrol to achieve the end for which a whole brigade has worn itself out. The possibility of rendering such service by acquiring information of vital importance should always be

in the mind of the leader of an independent reconnaissance.   He must never forget that his success
or failure may mean the success or failure of the
army to which he belongs.

CHAPTER II

The Scout

The scout has ever been a favorite hero of romance, and the very name carries with it a romantic idea of a man of exceptional courage and resource.

The public, which looks at all military affairs solely from the point of view of sentiment, regard a scout as one who is constantly in great danger, from which he escapes by the exercise of peculiar adroitness or by good fortune. In fact, it measures the fame of the scout by the amount of danger that he escapes. It is frequently forgotten that it is the scout's business to acquire information and that his reputation should depend upon his success in that line and not on his heroic adventures.

The scout who merely gets into danger and out again achieves nothing. He proves only that he is fitted for the first part of his duty—that is, to take care of himself in the immediate presence of the enemy.

It may be admitted that this first stage—the means to an end—is the fascinating part of scouting, and it is this which in the popular mind has obscured the final stage—the end to be obtained—the acquisition of information.

To carry out your work successfully as a scout, you will have to undergo continual risks and privations, and your training should be such that the chance of surviving these necessary dangers may be increased, remembering that the best scout is he who attains his mission while exposing himself as little as possible to danger.

Romance demands hair-breadth escapes and perils surmounted, but the commanding officer in the field wants information and will take much more interest in a dry narrative of facts about the enemy than in the most thrilling details of an unfruitful endeavor.

If you would be a successful scout, you must never lose sight of your ultimate object—information, and however enthralling you may find the pursuit of this object, you must remember that exciting adventures usually mean difficulties and delays and should be avoided when possible.

In the conduct of operations, as a scout you must be guided by the combination of qualities, courage and caution. Both of these are essential. The lack of either is fatal to efficiency. A timid and hesitating scout is of little use. A dead scout is of no use at all. A scout who has permitted himself to be captured by the enemy may be a positive danger.

The courage of the efficient scout must be of a fine temper. Mere hot-headed, blundering bravery, useful enough behind a bayonet, is out of place on a reconnaissance. Its exercise is the sure road to disaster. The scout should be of equable temperament, cool and undisturbed in the face of danger. His firm resolution to win out must be unmoved by difficulties and obstacles which are sure to be found. He must be content to play the game for its own sake, as it is likely enough that gallantry will be unseen by others and go unrecorded and unheralded.

Qualifications of a Scout Let us consider the qualifications that a man ought to possess in order to attain success as a scout:

1. He must be physically fit. Under this heading may be included: Such good eyesight as will enable him to see and distinguish objects of military value at a distance; good hearing, for he will be called upon to operate at night when this sense is far more valuable than any other: feet proportionate in size suitable to weight—the heavy man with a small foot is at a great disadvantage in getting over rough country as may be noted in good cross-country runners, who have large feet in proportion to their size and weight; litheness and agility to permit of quick movement from place to place, scaling barriers and climbing trees. A soldier who is subject to a recurrence of certain diseases, is useless as a scout.

2. He must be intelligent and trustworthy. With respect to the former, a man is of little value as a scout unless he possesses sufficient intelligence to be able to impart to others by means of a message or orally the information about the enemy that he has been able to secure. As to the latter, a man who is addicted to drink or who will allow himself to take a drink of intoxicating liquor while on duty is not suited for scout duty. The two positively will not mix.

3. He should be able to ride a horse and bicycle and be able to swim; even the infantry scout may

pick up a horse or a bicycle when he is in a hurry to get back with information. The ability to swim may save many miles of detour in looking for a ford or passage of a stream, or may be the means of escape with important information if pursuit is close.

4. He must be able to read and write. The scout will, in the course of his operations, come across many documents that may contain valuable information, and he must be able to read their contents so as to separate the valuable from the worthless. Much information that will be secured will have to be transmitted back to officers by means of a written message. The ability to write in a clear, legible hand is therefore necessary.

Possessing the above enumerated qualifications, the soldier can be taught:

1. Map reading to a sufficient extent to enable him to orient a map, find his own position and locate that of the enemy on it.

2. Elementary field sketching. He should be able to make rough pencil sketches showing the topographic details of localities of importance and to fill in roughly certain details of a section of map that may for the moment be important.

3. How to write a message.

4. Signaling.

5. Principles of security and information including the combined operations of a detachment of scouts with a patrol.

6. Methods of a reconnaissance.

7. Personal hygiene and first aid.

These are all very simple and easily learned if he will apply himself properly.

If you would be a successful scout, there are certain other qualities that you must attain for yourself. They are subjects which can be mastered only after assiduous application very much in your own way and of your own accord.

Among these subjects may be enumerated:

1. Courage and self-confidence.
2. The ability to find your way over unfamiliar country, that is, an eye for ground.
3. The use of eyes and ears.
4. The art of concealment.

Many men fail to measure up to the requirements because they only try to learn what they are shown and have not the ambition to practice themselves at other times.

When you were on the athletic squad at college or school and the trainer told you what you ought to eat and what you should not eat, and how much daily exercise you should take, do you remember how careful you were to follow his instructions to the letter, how you deprived yourself of just that one cigarette, how much practice and thought you gave to your specialty in order that you might fit yourself to win. That is the same process that you will have to pursue to make yourself efficient as a military scout.

CHAPTER III

Notes on Scouting

To be successful in the rôle of a scout, you must have a knowledge of military art and for further aids you must rely upon resolution, keen perception, and quick understanding. Without resolution, you will seldom gain a position to discover anything; without perception, you will fail to find that which lies within your view; and without understanding, you will be unable to grasp the meaning of that which you have found.

You must have plenty of that "never-say-die" quality that we Americans call "pep," which translated means alertness, wide-awakeness, stick-to-itiveness, and readiness to seize an opportunity.

Nervousness If you find yourself nervous about the enemy's scouts, just think how much more so they must be about you. If you know what to do and do it, your opponent is almost sure to get the worst of the encounter. When you discover a hostile scout lurking behind a bush, ask yourself whether, if you had the chance, you would change places with him. If you must answer in the affirmative, it should be your first object to improve your position, and this can rarely be accomplished except by moving forward or to a flank.

Finding Way The scout who loses his way not only imperils his own safety but the important interests depending upon his work, and in any case wastes *time*.

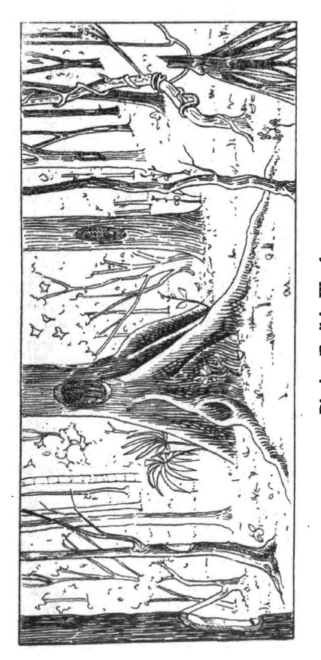

Blazing Trail in Woods.

In difficult country such as jungle, broken mountains, and ravines, it is a useful thing for you to make your own landmarks for finding your way. This may be accomplished by breaking small branches of trees, by blazing or cutting slices of bark from trees, piling up a few stones at selected places along your route, tying long grass into a knot, or drawing a distinct line across any trails that you did not follow. Such marks may also serve as guides to any others coming along your track.

A great assistance in finding your way in a strange country are landmarks or prominent features of any kind such as distant hills, towers, conspicuous trees, the line of railways, rivers, etc. Thus on starting on a reconnaissance, if you see a prominent mountain to the northward of you, it will serve as a guide without referring to the compass or to the sun. If you start from a church or other prominent building, it will be a guide or landmark for making your way back again later on. When you pass any conspicious object like a withered tree, a broken gate, a strangely shaped rock, keep it in mind so that should you have to return that way or want to send instructions to others who may want to find their way along that route, you can do so by following the chain of landmarks. On passing such landmarks, look back and see what their appearance is from the other side.

Capture   If you are captured by the enemy while scouting, your further services are lost to your cause, and you will probably be unable to transmit the information that you may have obtained of the enemy to your own forces. You must therefore keep a good lookout to your flanks and rear. You must frequently consider your immediate and ultimate line of retreat. As a general precaution, you should not retreat along the same line by which you made your way to the front but should as your reconnaissance progresses, make a selection of alternative lines of retreat and consider at each stage which of these lines is for the moment the most available and how in an emergency you would reach it, so that if surprised you may instantly turn in the right direction with a rough plan of escape already in your mind. The danger of surprise is the hesitation it usually causes, and if met confidently, it loses much of its effect.

Your security will depend upon your ability to recognize and estimate possible dangers. You must see the enemy before he sees you, and as an aid to accomplishing this, you should size up the situation from his point of view in order to make an estimate of where you will find him. As you advance, you should note the places where the enemy is most likely to be found either as an outpost or lookout position. You should be on the alert for every movement from that direction, for it is by that means that the presence of life is most easily detected. If your suspicions be directed to some definite locality, you should at once make up your mind to a line of action between two courses: either make the place the immediate object of your reconnaissance or avoid it altogether. Any middle course is accompanied by risks that are unnecessary to take.

Methods   Should you find it necessary to advance across a succession of open parallel ridges on one of which it is possible that you will find a patrol of the enemy, the procedure would normally be: Having made your way to the crest of the first ridge, observe

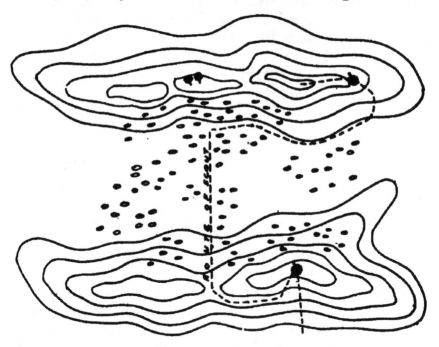

Reconnaissance of Parallel Ridges.

the second for signs of the enemy.   If you are unable to determine definitely whether it is occupied, assume that it is and proceed to out-maneuver your unseen opponent. If you want to get anywhere, you have to keep pushing along. Get up and cross the ridge taking advantage of any available cover, go down the hill, and when you reach the valley, move rapidly to a flank for several hundred yards and then go up the hill. There is usually a strip of ground at the bottom that is not visible from

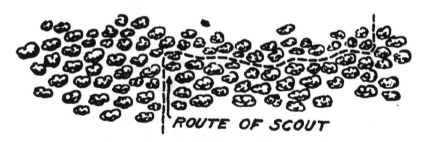

ROUTE OF SCOUT

the topographic crest of the hill and your move to the flank will be out of the range of vision of a concealed enemy. If the enemy is on the hill, he will probably be watching for you where you would have to come up had you continued on your course, and the diversion of attention will place you in a favorable position. (See cut.)

Never emerge from a woods into a clearing in prolongation of your route before entering the woods.   The enemy may be laying a trap for you, and if you appear at an unexpected point, his plans will be upset, and he will have to start all over again. This gives you a material advantage.   (See cut.)

Always assume any place which might conceal an enemy to be occupied until you have made certain that it is not, and do not pass without first reconnoitering it.

In approaching a locality where you think an enemy's scout may be in hiding, it may be well to act as if you saw something of him.   For example, you might stop suddenly, place your glasses to your eyes and motion as if you were signaling a companion to join you or point as if showing him something. If the enemy is there, the chances are that he will fire or sneak away, in either of which cases you will have carried out your design.

When you are sent back with a message by your patrol commander, be careful to take advantage of all available cover.   An enemy's patrol may have let your own patrol pass and is now disposed for the special purpose of intercepting messengers returning home with the information that has been gained.

You should never enter an enclosure, artificial or natural, until you have made doubly sure that your retreat by your original entrance is secure or that there are one or more other outlets that can be used in an emergency. Never enter a house alone. Keep away from farm houses and corrals.   Do not use a road or trail with a high cliff on one side and an impassable water course on the other; get up on top of the cliff.   Avoid fields where there is a succes--

sion of wire fences to climb, for you will lose time in getting over them, and you present a good target for a marksman while so doing. Should you have been mounted and left your horse to continue on foot, he should be in a position where he can be quickly mounted and the start made at a gallop. Should a bicycle be used, it should be left facing in the direction of your retreat and at the top of a rise from which point advantage can be taken of a flying start. If you are working on foot, it is usually best to make for broken ground or woods where a horseman would be at a disadvantage.

When moving at night, keep in the hollows as much as possible so as to be able to watch the sky line all around you.

When advancing toward an opponent, it is better to have the sun shining in your face than to have it shining directly behind you. In the former case, there will be few shadows cast by your person, while in the latter, your front will be all shadow darkly outlined against almost any background that may be behind you.

If you can possibly avoid it, do not move across an open space where the enemy may be able to spot you from a position on your flank. Any movement of this kind that you may make by a flank will almost be sure to be observed.

It will often be well when firing over a wall or embankment to place a few hats several yards to the flank of your actual location. They may serve to draw many of the enemy's bullets away from you. This trick is well known to experienced scouts,

Firing Over a Wall.

for it is a well known fact that one will aim at what can be seen. For example, in our field firing if there is a figure that is less visible than the others through having a blending background, the chances are about five to one that the figure will not receive a hit.

In dodging an enemy around the outside of a house or building, always work around contra-clockwise, for you will then be able to shoot around the corner without exposing yourself as much as your opponent.

CHAPTER IV

Concealment

It is the duty of the scout to keep himself and his intentions concealed from the enemy as much as possible. This art of concealment may be accomplished to a great extent by the use of ordinary common sense; by the proper use of crest lines, summits of hills and the avoidance of open ground; by the exercise of caution when moving; by remaining absolutely motionless when halted; by the judicious selection of observation posts; and by taking advantage of darkness.

Common Sense Unless we see some reason for exercising caution, we are likely to disdain concealment and move along the line of least resistance. As a scout you must regard every feature of the terrain as a possible hiding place of the enemy, ready in waiting to capture or kill you, and conduct your operations accordingly. You will probably gain twice as much information of the foe if he is ignorant of the fact that he is being watched.

If, despite all your precautions, the enemy does discover you, it may be well to pretend that you have not seen him, or it may be a good ruse to pretend that you have friends close by and make signals for them to join you.

Do not place yourself in a position where there will be great contrast between your uniform and your background. Make the two blend together whenever possible and thus add to your invisibility. With your olive drab uniform, trees and bushes in leaf and drab-colored earth and rocks make good backgrounds.

Study the enemy's methods of operation, and you will soon be able to estimate pretty accurately what he will do under certain conditions. You can then make your plans accordingly.

You must be careful to have no article about you that will shine or flash in the sunlight. Your accouterments and equipment are all designed to prevent this very thing. Eye glasses may give a flash and should not be worn while scouting on a bright day, when in close contact with the enemy.

Use of Crest Lines, etc. In making use of ridge lines and summits of hills as observation points, be very careful not to show yourself on the top or sky line.

On reaching a high place, it is a great temptation to get on top and take a good look around, especially when you see no signs of the enemy beyond. The enemy will be watching just such places from his concealed positions, and because you do not see him immediately, do not jump at the conclusion that he is not in the vicinity. Most of the enemies that we are likely to encounter are people that are adepts in scouting and keeping themselves hidden while on such service. The method recommended is as follows: On reaching a point near the top of the crest, lie down and crawl on all fours. On reaching the top raise the head very slowly, inch by inch, until you get the required view beyond. **If you** see any of the enemy, make the necessary **observa-**tion in the furtherance of your mission. **Remain** perfectly still. After you have completed your observation, lower the head inch by inch and retire. Any sudden or quick movement on the skyline would be almost sure to reveal your position to an alert enemy, even at a considerable distance.

Never move in the open when you can possibly avoid it. Take a longer way around and stay under cover.

Exercise of Caution When Moving You should take advantage of all possible cover. Move along hedges, fences, behind embankments, and in water courses. Should it become absolutely necessary to operate in open country, make your way from cover to cover at a rapid gait while in the open and conduct your observations while at a halt. There is scarcely any piece of ground that will not furnish some cover for a single scout, and it will pay you to seek it out.

Remaining Motionless When Halted The importance of controlling the body to absolute stillness cannot be over-estimated. It is the natural endowment of many wild animals which cannot be acquired by man without much practice. If you keep perfectly motionless, you will remain unobserved for a long time at very close range in a place where concealment would seem impossible.

It may be interesting for you to make an experiment along these lines. Post yourself at some point where the cover is not specially good. Remain absolutely motionless and see how many persons pass without observing you.

Selection of Observation Posts Be careful in the selection of your observation posts. Choose some unlikely spot that affords a good lookout, good concealment, and a line of escape. You will naturally seek the high points from which to observe the country and look out for the enemy. These are the very places that the enemy will be watching most closely so that you must be doubly cautious in occupying them.

A tower usually affords a good lookout station, but if the enemy discovers you, all he has to do is to guard the base, and you cannot get away with the information that you have obtained.

Ordinarily the roof of a house will be found almost as good as a tower, and there are usually several routes by which you may be able to make your get away in case of discovery. Avoid ridge, or keep close to chimneys.

Trees have about the same disadvantage as towers, but you may be able to conceal yourself more effectually in the foliage and thus escape detection. When approaching and climbing trees, be careful to leave no tell-tale tracks by which you may be trailed. The experienced scout is always on the lookout for tracks, and muddy foot marks on tree trunks may give away your position. When observing from trees, get up near the top and stand on a limb close

Use of Ridge of House.

Means for Climbing Large Tree.

in beside the trunk of the tree or lie flat on a limb. Where the branches hang low it may be possible to climb up on the outer limbs and thus eliminate the possibility of leaving footmarks at the bottom of the tree.

You can cut down a small tree so that it will lean against a large one too big to climb by ordinary methods.

You should always make full use of one post of observation before leaving it for another. You may be able to lie in one place observing the enemy for a considerable length of time undetected and then be chased by him within a few minutes after leaving it.

In looking out through a bush, it may be well to break off a leafy branch and hold it before the face.

The Turks proved themselves adepts at concealment during the Gallipoli campaign when they covered their snipers with the branches of trees and posted them in advantageous positions. It is probably safe to say that fifty escaped discovery for every one who was discovered.

Darkness   At night, the enemy will expect to find you along roads and trails. If you have in peace times practiced finding your way across country at night, you will not be dependent on them, and you will find your value as a scout considerably increased.

At night, you will make use of the deep shadows cast by trees and bushes. Keep as much as possible on low ground and in ditches, etc., so that you are

Holding Bush in Front of Face.

down in the dark, while the enemy who comes near will be visible on the sky line or lined out against the high ground.

When in danger of being discovered, lie close to the ground and remain perfectly quiet.   An enemy scout may come within a few feet of you without discovering your presence.

At night the scout on foot has every advantage over the mounted scout.   It is then difficult to get horses over rough country.   They are usually nervous and may, by the noise they make, give your position away.

The flash of a lighted match on a dark night may be seen for a distance of some 900 yards, and the glow from a cigarette is distinguishable for more than 300 yards.

CHAPTER V

Seeing and Hearing

Nature has endowed you with two senses, the judicious use of which are necessary to successful scouting. These are sight and hearing. Both may, with practice, be developed to a point of efficiency that you would hardly imagine possible.

Sight Training With regard to teaching yourself the art of what we shall term for want of a better word, "scout seeing," go to some good lookout point equipped with a pair of field glasses. Look at distant objects, first with the naked eye, using your hands Indian fashion and see what you can make out. Follow this by verifying your estimation with the glasses. Then take your field glasses and reverse the operation. Select some distant object with the aid of the glasses and then gaze at it until you can see it with the naked eye. Note that moving objects are more easily detected than those that remain motionless. The knack of using field glasses is easily acquired with a little practice, and you should not neglect this essential element of your training as a scout. It may be the means of saving your life or the acquirement of most valuable information in the course of your operations.

The savage almost invariably has the knack of quick eyesight developed to a high degree. He has also by continual practice trained his eyes to see for great distances.

Long Distance Reconnoitering.

In long distance reconnoitering, lie flat on your stomach, place your elbows firmly on the ground, rest your cheeks on your hands so placed as to shade your eyes and limit your front of vision. Fix your gaze upon the distant object and watch it intently. You will be surprised to see how the details will clear up. This is known as the Indian method. It was by employing this method that Bloody Knife, one of General Custer's Indian scouts located Sitting Bull's camp on the Little Big Horn at a distance of 12 miles. He first discovered the smoke ascending from their fires and later was able to make out ponies grazing in the valley.

Another method of limiting your field of vision is to cut off the upper part by the brim of your hat and the lower by placing the hands under the eyes as shown in the illustration.

Distinguishing Objects You will be able on a clear day to distinguish objects as follows:

Church spires and towers........... 8 to 10 miles.
Wind mills and large houses........ 5 to 7 miles.
Windows and chimneys............ 4,000 yards.
Telegraph poles................... 1,500 yards.

Troops will be visible at about 2,000 yards, at which distance a mounted man looks like a mere speck; at 1,200 yards infantry can be distinguished from cavalry. At 1,000 yards, a line of infantry looks like a black line on the ground; at 600 yards, the files of a squad can be counted. At 500 yards, men's heads and the shape of their headgear can be

Limiting the Vision.

seen. The larger, brighter or better lighted an object is, the nearer it seems. An object seems nearer when it has a dark background than when it had a light one, and closer on a clear day than when it is raining, snowing, foggy, or when the atmosphere is filled with smoke. An object looks farther off when you are facing the sun than when you have your back to it. A smooth expanse of snow, grain fields, or water makes the distances seem shorter than they really are.

A moving man is easy to see, but one who stands stock still and is not silhouetted against a contrasting background is very difficult to pick up with the naked eye.

Sound travels at the rate of about 1,120 feet per second. You will be able to estimate the distance to a hostile force by noting the time that elapses between the flashes of the gun and the time the report is heard. The number of seconds multiplied by 1,120 will give you the distance fairly accurately.

At night when there is profound stillness, the beat of a horse's hoofs on the road, or the ordinary tones of a man's voice will carry a long distance compared with the same sounds by day. If you will place your ear to the ground, or a stick resting on the ground, or on a fence post carrying wires, you will be able to perceptibly increase the distance that such sounds may be heard.

CHAPTER VI

Signs of the Enemy

As you make your way through hostile country, you should be continually on the lookout for the enemy or any signs of him, such as rising dust, glitter of arms in the sunlight, smoke from fires and at night the flash of a match.

Often when passing through jungle or hill country, a thin wisp of smoke, the flash of a rifle barrel, bayonet or other bright weapon in the sunlight will reveal the enemy's whereabouts to the alert eye of the scout.

Troops on March From the dust raised by a column of troops on the march, you will not only be able to determine the direction of the march but the strength and composition of the troops forming the column. With infantry, the dust is low and thick; with cavalry, the dust is higher and if they are moving rapidly the upper part of the cloud is thinner and disappears more quickly than in the case of infantry. The dust raised by artillery and wagon trains is unequal in height and disconnected. By estimating the length of a line of dust and noting its character, the strength and composition of the column can be fairly accurately estimated by allowing one yard for each two infantrymen marching in column of squads and one yard for each mounted man and 20 yards for each gun, caisson, or wagon. If you are not able to see

40

the dust from the entire column, you will have to estimate the strength from the time it takes to pass a given point. Infantry moving in column of squads will pass a point at a rate of about 200 men per minute; cavalry in fours at a walk at about 150 or if in rear of infantry about 100 per minute, cavalry at a trot, about 260. Four guns or caissons or wagons will consume a minute in passing. If you are close enough actually to see the column, this method is very accurate, but if you have to depend entirely upon dust clouds, you must be a keen observer with experience to arrive at anything like a definite conclusion as to numbers and composition.

The noise made by a strong column of troops on the march is distinct and continuous; that of a small body feeble and interrupted. The distance at which you will be able to hear these sounds depends upon the nature of the ground marched over, the direction of the wind, and the presence or absence of other sounds. On a calm night, you will be able to hear a column of infantry marching on a hard road a distance of 500 or 600 yards away; a troop of cavalry at a walk, 600 to 700 yards; cavalry at a trot or gallop and artillery or wagon trains at 900 to 1,000 yards.

Tracks You will obtain much information about the enemy from the ground at your feet. You will be able to tell whether he has been over the country. You can follow him up by his tracks whether he be a large force or merely a patrol. If the road is evenly trodden, infantry is on the march.

If there are many points of horse shoes, the column also contained cavalry. The wheel tracks will indicate to you the class of artillery that has passed provided you are familiar with the enemy's armament.

In following up tracks, do not look at the ones at your feet but cast your eye some distance ahead. It is easier to follow tracks when moving towards the sun than with the sun behind you.

A man walking places the whole of the flat of his foot equally on the ground, the prints a little less than a yard distance between them. When running, the toes of the foot prints are deeply indented in the ground, and they are ordinarily more than a yard apart. Do not be fooled by a man walking backwards to conceal the direction of his march. The age of a track can be determined fairly accurately by close examination of the edges to determine to what extent they have been worn off by wind action and the drying up of the damp soil that was indented when the track was made.

You ought to know at a glance the gait at which a horse that you are tracking was going and how long since he passed. At a walk, the hoof marks will be in pairs, the hind foot marks more or less overlapping those made by the front foot. The pairs will be about a yard apart. At a trot, the hoof marks will be in pairs the same as at a walk but about 4 feet apart, and the marks will be more deeply indented in the earth. At a gallop, the hoof marks will be separate and about $3\frac{1}{2}$ feet apart. In a fast walk or trot, the hind hoof marks will be found in front of those made by the fore feet instead of over them. A freshly made track shows sharp edges, and the ground usually shows signs of moisture where it has been broken. In about 15 minutes, the moisture will have disappeared.

Bicycle tracks are more wobbly going up hill than when coming down.

Estimating Strength   The method of estimating the strength of a force by counting bivouac fires cannot be recommended. The lighting of dummy fires is one of the time-honored artifices of war. If a commander desires to make a show of strength, he may light dummy fires to give the opposing scouts the impression that he has a stronger force than he really has. If he is strong and does not want the fact revealed, he may forbid the lighting of fires, so there is no real basis for calculation. The same fires may serve ten men one night and fifty the next.

The strength of a command in bivouac must be estimated by the number of organizations observed, so that you must have a unit with which you are familiar aptly termed the "unit of estimation." In other words, you must know the tactical units of the enemy, company, battalion, regiment, troop, squadron, and battery, and count the units that are visible from your observation point. You should know the physical appearance of the units of estimation so as to be able to distinguish them. If you have all of the knowledge about the units of your own army, it will be a simple process to apply it to the units of the enemy's forces.

The rumbling of vehicles, cracking of whips, neighing of horses, braying of mules and barking of dogs, often indicate the arrival or departure of troops within the enemy's lines. If the noise remains in the same place and new fires are lighted, it is probable that reinforcements have arrived. If the noise grows more indistinct troops are probably withdrawing.

During the campaign in the Philippines in 1899, we could always tell when any considerable body of the enemy were in the vicinity even if they had not been reported. Their presence was revealed by the distant barking of dogs and the extreme restlessness of the animals in the command, especially the American mules. Our scouts were often able to trace the movements of a body of Filipinos that were hidden in the jungle, by the barking of dogs along the route.

System of Protection   There is one detail of information about the enemy that you ought to be able to report with accuracy, and that is the efficiency of his system of protection. It is with the hostile covering troops that you will come into immediate contact, and you will be able to discover whether the outposts are vigilant or careless, and whether the patrols are aggressive or timid. This knowledge may be of supreme importance. A slackness in the enemy's outpost line which permits you to make important observations may also enable your commander to achieve a victory by surprise.

CHAPTER VII

Patrols

The question will always arise as to whether it will be better to employ a scout or pair of scouts on a certain mission or whether a patrol had best be sent out. There are no hard and fast rules that may be invoked in arriving at a decision but there are certain principles that may be applied and when reconnaissance enterprises are to be undertaken the condition should be examined closely. The scout or pair of scouts would as a rule be preferred when concealment is highly essential, and usually when concealment, though not essential, is possible throughout the reconnaissance or when the enemy habitually conducts his reconnaissance with strong patrols and scouts have a better chance of eluding him.

In the following cases a patrol should be employed: When information has to be sent in at intervals; when it is desired to capture prisoners; when concealment is deemed impossible; when the reconnaissance is to be extended over such a period of time that relief of scouts will be necessary; when an urgent mission has been assigned and it is necessary to push through the enemy's covering troops.

If possible the individual preferences of the most efficient scouts should be considered. Some men lose self-confidence if attached to a patrol and are limited in their actions by the direction of the patrol leader, others dislike the responsibility of uncon-

trolled action.   In some cases it may be advisable
to employ a patrol for the first part of the reconnaissance and at a certain point break up into scouting parties of a single scout or pair of scouts.

These are only general rules and cannot be
followed blindly.   The circumstances of each
occasion must be taken into consideration in
arriving at a decision.

Duties
The first duty of a patrol is
to get information and information is greatly increased in value
if the enemy does not know that it has been obtained.
The patrol is required, primarily, to discover
whether or not the enemy is in a certain locality.
This information is only useful to the officer who
sent the patrol out.   It is, therefore, the next duty
of the patrol to get the information back as soon as
possible especially when the enemy is met.

Next of importance in the duties of the patrol
is to continue to observe the enemy when once discovered, to follow him up and ascertain the direction taken if he retires or to fall back if he advances
in strength, endeavoring to keep even with him on
a flank.   The enemy is certain to send out scouts
to his front but may neglect his flanks.

Boldness must be tempered with caution.   It is
worse than useless to obtain information if you can
not get it back where it will do some good.   A
little information sent in in time to be of use is
clear gain to your side.   A patrol that finds out all
about the enemy and ends up by falling into the
hands of the enemy is a dead loss, not only in men

but in time, as other patrols may have to be sent
out to get the same information on which important
decisions may depend.

Strength The strength of the patrol
depends upon the mission which
has been assigned to it and the
probable number of messages that will have to be
sent back. A greater number of men than are
necessary to accomplish the work at hand is simply
a drag on the patrol commander and the greater
will be the chance for the enemy to discover your
movements. On the other hand, if the patrol is too
weak, the enemy lying concealed, may allow two or
three men to walk into an ambush and take a chance
on bagging them, whereas they would probably open
fire at a longer range on a greater number. The
patrol consisting of a leader and six scouts seems to
be very appropriate for ordinary reconnaissance
work. There will be an advance man, a man for
each flank, one for the get-away-man and two to
march with the patrol leader as main body to be
employed to relieve the covering men who may
come in with verbal reports, or to be employed in
sending messages back.

Composition The ideal patrol would be
one composed of trained individual scouts commanded by an
officer or noncommissioned officer who is himself
qualified as a scout.

It is desirable when operating in foreign lands
that at least one member should be able to speak
the language of the country.

Commander   The commander should have rank in order that he may have authority, for his decisions must be final in every detail of combined procedure. Furthermore, there are instances when it is necessary to impart to the leader of a patrol, information of a highly secret nature, perhaps connected with military plans, information which can only be entrusted to an officer or noncommissioned officer of proved discretion.

Equipment   Besides his regular equipment the patrol commander should have field glasses, compass, watch, wire-cutter, pencils, book of field message blanks and if available a map of the country over which the patrol is to operate. Each member of the patrol should in addition to his regular equipment have a wire-cutter, field glasses, and compass. At least one member should carry a combination flag kit for wig-wag and semaphore signaling.

If a member of a patrol is taken prisoner at any time the only information that the enemy should be able to secure from him is his name and rank. It is therefore necessary that everything that would give any other information should be discarded.

In jungle country there should be at least two bolos in the patrol.

Instructions   Officers sending out patrols will give them instructions which will include:

1. Information of the enemy, and information of our own troops, especially with respect to any other patrols that may have been sent out.

2. The mission of the patrol. That is the general direction in which it is to go and the object for which the patrol is being sent out.

3. How long the patrol is to remain out so far as it is possible to determine in advance.

4. Where messages are to be sent.

These instructions may take the following form which would be modified in every case to meet the tactical situation existing at the time.

Captain: "A detachment of the enemy bivouacked last night at *a* and small parties are suspected in the vicinity of *b*. Sergeant B's patrol is moving out by the *c-d* trail and will cover the country to the south thereof. You will take a patrol of six men and move out in the direction of *a* and find out what you can about the enemy.

"Remain out until darkness prevents further reconnaissance.

"Send reports to me at Support No. 2."

The patrol commander must be sure that he understands his instructions. If he has the slightest doubt about any of them he should ask questions until it is completely cleared up.

When there is no reason to the contrary each member of the patrol should know the mission on which it has been sent out so that if anything should happen to the leader or the patrol meet with disaster each man who has escaped may individually do what he can to obtain the desired information.

Preparations Before going out the patrol commander will make a careful inspection of his patrol to satisfy himself that the members are in suitable condition for the duty to be performed. He will see that each man is properly armed, has the requisite amount of ammunition, and that none are sick, footsore or intoxicated. He will assure himself that their accouterment is so arranged as not to glisten in the sunlight nor rattle when they walk or move, and that no man has anything about him that will afford the enemy any valuable information.

In the presence of the officer sending out the patrol he will go over his orders and instructions, giving the men all the information he has of the enemy and his own troops, state the mission of the patrol in order that all may know what they are going out to accomplish, and he will follow this with a statement of his general plan for carrying it out. If the members of the patrol are all selected and well instructed scouts the following will not be required but this is the exception rather than the rule. If the men are not already familiar with them he will explain the signals by which interior communication between the members of the patrol is maintained (see chapter X). He will impress upon the members of the patrol the necessity for concealment, warn them about firing their pieces and caution them that they must neither talk nor smoke. He will designate the first place of assembly to which all the members of the patrol proceed in case the patrol is broken up and each man has to shift for himself for the time being. These assembly points are changed from time to time as the patrol advances. He will designate a member of the patrol to take command in case an accident befalls

himself. He will then compare his watch with that
of the officer sending out the patrol and is ready to
start.

Starting If the patrol on going out
passes through an outpost line
the commander should confer
with the outguard commander nearest his line of
advance, getting any information that he may
have about the enemy and the ground in front,
inform him how many men are in the patrol, the
general direction in which he intends to go, what
time he intends to return (especially if the hour of
return be after dark) and arrange a signal by which
he may be identified, in order that the sentinel may
receive instructions in regard to the matter. The
outguard commander will probably accompany
the patrol as far as his sentinels and give them
instructions regarding the patrol.

If the enemy's scouts have been able to locate
the outpost they will probably be watching the line
of sentinels and would at once notice a patrol
moving out over open ground and be prepared to
deal with the situation. When the patrol reaches
cover the movement of the men can no longer be
observed by the enemy and he will be uncertain as
to where they are going and will probably get
uneasy about his own safety. If the patrol selects
a line of advance which is covered from view during
the first part of the operation but emerges later into
open ground, any hostile scouts who may be on the
lookout will not be able to discover the movement
so soon but will be able to watch the later stages of

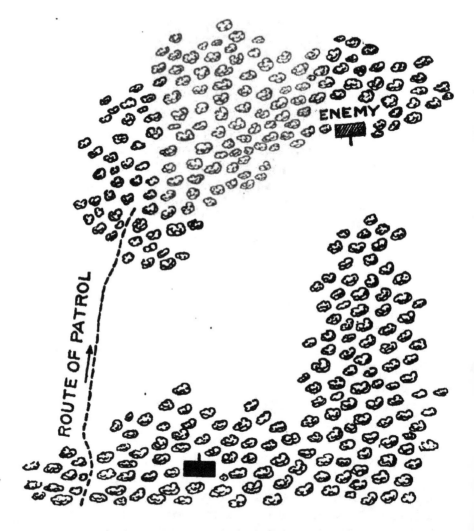

Patrol Starting from Outpost Line.

the advance and prepare to evade or waylay the patrol. It appears therefore that when there is no line of advance which is covered the whole way from the outpost line to the end of the first lap of the patrol and there is a choice of two lines, one of which is covered for the last part, it is best to select the latter.

Formation It is impossible to lay down any hard and fast rule governing the formation and conduct of the operations of a patrol. Each situation will have to be worked out by itself and will vary with the topography of the country, the object of the reconnaissance and the action of the enemy.

If the patrol advances in one body a hostile patrol may allow them to approach and then ambuscade and capture them. If the patrol advances in an extended line, capture is rendered much more difficult, but each man will be acting more or less independently and it will be most difficult for the patrol leader to control the operations.

The patrol will assume the general formation of a column of troops on the march with its covering detachments, that is it will have an advance guard, a main body, flankers and a rear guard. These several elements may be represented by only one man, but the principles are exactly the same as if a large force were being employed. The advance guard is necessary to give warning of the approach of the enemy. The flankers are necessary to watch towards the flanks and prevent the enemy from ambuscading the patrol or working around to its

SUGGESTED FORMATION FOR PATROLS

3 Men   4 Men   5 Men

6 Men   7 Men

Symbol	Role	Symbol	Role	Symbol	Role
♂	POINT	☿	SPARE MAN	♂	RIGHT FLANKER
♂	LEADER	♀	GET-AWAY-MAN	♂	LEFT FLANKER

rear, unobserved and cutting off its line of retreat. The main body is necessary to back up the advance guard and protect him. The rear guard is the get-away-man so that in case the patrol is fired into or captured at least one man has a good chance to escape and carry the news back to the officer who sent the patrol out.

When a small patrol is advancing along a road which is more or less winding and has brush and trees along the side, the "Boni point" formation will usually meet the requirements. In this formation, the leading man walks along the side of the road close up to the brush. The next man follows him at a distance of about 25 yards walking on the opposite side of the road. The remaining men follow at varying distances on alternate sides of the road. The rear or "get-away-man" should march at least 75 yards in rear of his next preceding man. Flankers are sent out when necessary.

Some authorities advocate that the patrol commander march as the advance man of the patrol. This is not believed to be good tactics. He should be centrally located so that he will be able to control the operations of his patrol. The patrol leader has been selected for this particular line of work. The officer who sent him out is depending upon him to carry out the mission upon which he has been sent and to get information back. He should not, therefore, needlessly make himself a target for the enemy marksmen who may be lying in concealment at the turn of the road or trail. If he is the leading man he will be so busily occupied with the task of

observation that he will have little time available
for conducting the operations of the other members
of the patrol. Furthermore, if anything happens
at the front that needs his attention he can go there
in a very short space of time.

The formation of the patrol must be elastic, that
is the various elements should be able tempor-
arily to diverge or alter speed without throwing the
formation out of gear. A flank scout cannot carry
out his duties properly if he is obliged to conform
rigidly to another's movements. He must conform
generally to the movements of the commander.

**Communi-
cation**   The ordinary communication
between the patrol leader and
members of his patrol is accomplished by means of signals. No
formation, however, is entirely satisfactory which
does not provide for verbal communication between
the two and thus far no set of signals has been
devised that will convey the details of information
and it is often in the details that the importance
lies. In case the detached scout has information
which he desires to impart to the patrol commander
he signals: "Have Important Information" (see
chapter on signals and signaling) in which case
the patrol commander either joins the scout to
make observations for himself or sends one of his
spare men to relieve the scout in order that he
may come in and make a verbal report. The scout
then becomes a spare man until he is required to
go out to the relief of another scout. This method
gives complete communication throughout the

patrol at all times at a great saving of time and effort.

Conduct of the Patrol The patrol moves, in proper formation, cautiously but not timidly, taking advantage of all available cover, seeking in every way to see without being seen. It halts frequently to listen and make careful observation of the surroundings.

As the patrol advances to the front each scout should individually make a mental note of such landmarks as will enable him to find his own way back. In close country such objects as peculiarly formed trees, rocks, etc., should be remembered. Often such objects will have an entirely different appearance from the other side.

Except at night the patrol should not move on roads. Villages and inhabited places should not, as a rule, be entered. This does not mean that observation of these should be neglected. On the contrary, important roads are the very ones that must be most carefully watched for they are the routes that will be followed by any forces of the enemy whose movements are really worth reporting.

The patrol should not halt for a prolonged rest before its return unless circumstances render it absolutely necessary to do so. In such case it should rest in concealment in some place which offers advantages for defense and from which retreat may be easily effected. The position chosen should not be near any habitation. During the day it should be on high ground from which an extensive view can be obtained.   At night it should be on low ground so as to bring persons approaching into view on the sky line.

Whenever the patrol has to halt in a hollow or in any place where the view is limited one or more men must be sent to some higher ground to keep a lookout and prevent surprise.   The patrol leader should give careful instructions in regard to the duty and make sure that the men occupying the observation posts understand what they are to do.

A patrol on high ground has considerable moral and material advantage over one on low ground. The men can see more of the country, their line of retreat is safer, and they can run down hill faster than they can run up hill.   The only disadvantage is that they are more exposed to the view of hostile scouts, but this may be regulated by adopting the proper formation and employing the necessary precautions.

The manner of reconnoitering different kinds of ground depends upon the circumstances of each individual case, and no rigid rules can be prescribed. There are, however, certain general methods that have stood the test of centuries of warfare that may be stated.

Whenever the patrol has to move parallel to a ridge it will be necessary to know what is on the other side of it. In this case the nearest flanker would move along on the near side of the ridge and work his way to the crest at intervals to get a look to the other side.   In no event will he march along the crest where he would be silhouetted against the sky line.

If it should be necessary for the patrol to cross an open space lying between two woods, under the possible observation of a distant enemy there are three methods that are available; to cross, man by man in succession; to cross in one body; to cross simultaneously, but dispersed. Of these the first is not recommended for of all forms of movement, that which. is most likely to attract the eye is a recurring one. A single movement `may be seen but may be at an end before the mind of the observer has fully grasped its significance and he may be left in doubt as to whether or not he has really seen anything. A repetition of the movement confirms his suspicions and brings certainty. The difficult passage should be effected by the whole patrol simultaneously. Whether they should move in a body or dispersed depends upon the light and the background. If the enemy be not very near, closed bodies, if moving slowly, will often escape observation or if observed will be difficult to identify. In a failing light, men widely extended may effect the crossing unnoticed. If the distance be very short and the light good a quick rush may offer the best prospects.

When confronted by a series of ridges lying across the line of advance of the patrol there is always a possibility of having been observed by the enemy from his position on a succeeding ridge and he may prepare an ambuscade. Therefore on reaching the cover of the valley lying between the two ridges make a flank move to the right or left and cross the next ridge at some other point than that in prolongation of the original line of advance. This same procedure should be employed by the patrol when passing through a strip of woods.

If advancing near a road, when the patrol comes to a cross road or road fork, it will halt. One of the spare men with the patrol commander is sent out to form a connecting file for the flanker. The latter pushes down the cross road for the necessary distance, usually to the first turn. If nothing suspicious is seen the flanker returns to his normal position, the connecting file comes in and the patrol pushes on. If anything suspicious is seen the connecting file joins the flanker, gets the information and takes it to the patrol commander, the flanker remaining in observation.

In the reconnaissance of heights one of several methods may be employed. If the patrol is large enough to admit it one or two men climb the slope on either flank of the line of advance, keeping in sight of the patrol if possible. After their reconnaissance is completed the patrol may occupy the heights, being careful to avoid the sky line.

Another method that may be employed is for the patrol commander to draw in his flankers close and halt. Then send two men directly up the hill to make a preliminary reconnaissance keeping them covered by the rifles of the remaining members of the patrol. There may be an advantage in making a practice of scouting from the flank of a patrol for if it has been observed by the enemy and an ambush prepared the enemy's arrangements will probably have been made with a view to meeting a direct advance and any attempt on his part at rearrangement is likely enough to lead to his detection. So that in the reconnaissance of an isolated hill the patrol may swing to a flank and have the examination made by the flanker nearest the hill. The illustration will show this method.

The reconnaissance of defiles may be accomplished if time permits by swinging the patrol to a flank and having one of the flankers make the preliminary

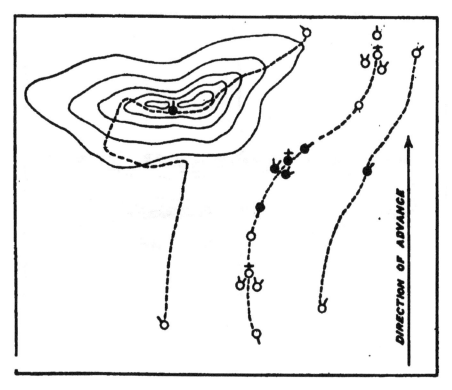

Reconnaissance of an Isolated Hill.

examination as illustrated in the case of an isolated hill above, or the heights on either side may be reconnoitered before the main body approaches. If the heights are inaccessible or time is urgent the patrol pushes through in "Boni point" formation at a rapid gait without flankers and the distances considerably increased.

The passage of a patrol across a bridge over an unfordable stream may be effected as follows:

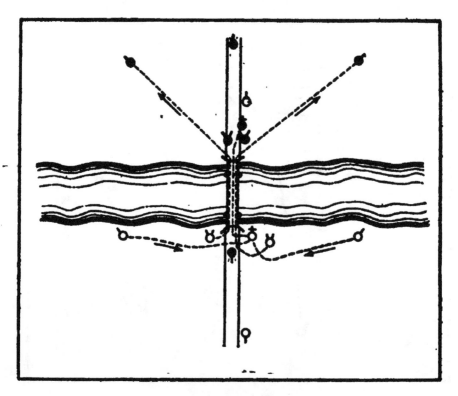

Patrol Crossing Bridge.

Approach the bridge in normal formation. Have the flankers halt and remain in position. Push the leading man across at double time and have him make a hasty reconnaissance covered by the rifles of the patrol leader and the two men with him. When he has signaled that all is apparently clear send the other two men across and have them move out to the right and left as flankers and as soon as they gain the intervals draw in the original flankers and have them follow. The "get-away-man" brings up the rear. See illustration.

The daylight passage of woods by a patrol requires considerable caution. The patrol enters in skirmishing order, the intervals being as great as may be consistent with mutual observation and support. Where the wood is fairly open the patrol should extend intervals and where it is close they should be decreased. On arriving at clearings or the farther edge of the woods the patrol will halt and make a careful reconnaissance before passing out into the open. Where the woods are so dense that the extended order formation is not practicable the advance along a road or trail may be conducted in the "Boni point" formation with two men in the point for it is likely enough if the enemy be met under such conditions only one or two men on each side will be able to come into action at a time, and if the two men are on the point they will be an even match for the enemy. The "get-away-man" must be kept far enough to the rear so that he will not become involved in the first affray. In advancing along roads and trails through woods or dense

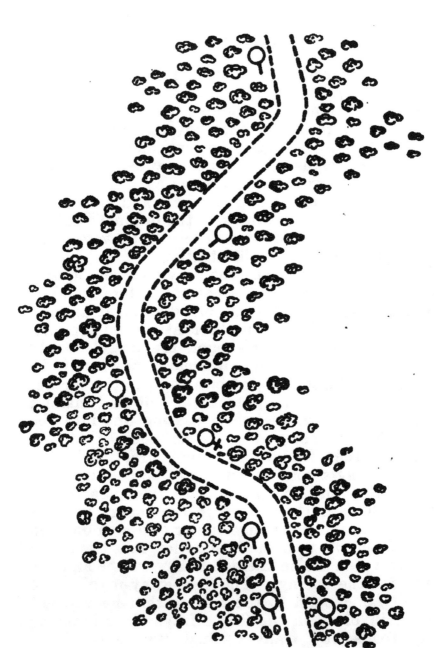

Boni Point Formation; Patrol Passing through Dense Woods.

jungle the patrol must be especially careful in approaching points where the route makes a sharp turn to the flank for it is at these angles the enemy has his best opportunity to take you by surprise and bring more rifles into action than you can.

The exterior of inclosures (gardens, parks, etc.), are first carefully examined to make sure that the enemy are not concealed behind one of the fences. The interior is then examined but not entered except under most exceptional circumstances.

When a house or farm building is approached by a patrol it is first carefully reconnoitered from a distance and then approached either by the direct method or by swinging a flank and having the nearest flanker make the examination the remainder of the patrol remaining concealed in observation and in such position as to cover the men engaged in the reconnaissance. If it is found necessary to enter two men approach each of the front and back doors, one man enters each door while the other remains outside on guard.

The patrol will not remain in the vicinity of habitations any longer than is absolutely necessary. When they leave they will proceed by a route other than that which they will eventually take, move out on it a sufficient distance to deceive any people who may be watching them and then get in on their proper line of advance.

When a village is seen to be in possession of the enemy the patrol must be content to reconnoitre it from the outside. If the presence of the enemy is not apparent, necessary precautions should be taken in entering. It may be reconnoitered by the direct method as in the case of heights or the examination may be made from a flank by diverting the direction of the patrol. The old idea of pushing through the main street with flankers out on the side streets should not be employed unless it is absolutely certain that no enemy are in the village.

The above are merely suggestions as to how the reconnaissance of various features may be accompished. The method that may be appropriate in one case might not be at all suitable in another. The patrol commander will have to work out a solution to each problem as it confronts him. If he has a knowledge of the general methods that experience has taught soldiers through the past generation he can easily apply the modification necessary to accomplish his object.

Encountering the Enemy The real work of the patrol begins when it touches upon the enemy. All other formations and methods are merely means by which the patrol may be enabled to reach a point where information of real value may be obtained. The commander wants information of the enemy's main forces, his numbers, composition and dispositions.

If a small hostile patrol is discovered it is generally better to remain in concealment and let it pass, than to attack. The capture of an entire patrol, advancing in proper formation, is a most difficult operation. One may almost say that it cannot be accomplished without firing. The noise thus created will doubtless be heard by the enemy and he will take further precautions by sending out stronger covering detachments and thus create a screen that will be impracticalbe for a small patrol to penetrate.

The matter of avoiding an enemy's patrol is easier said than done. We must give the enemy's patrol credit for being on the alert and for having such a knowledge of tactics that he will do the reasonably proper thing. If he sees one member of our patrol the difficulty of avoiding him will be doubly increased. Some of the members of the patrol may have to fall back or move by a flank a short distance to get cover. The decision will have to be made quickly and the necessary signals given and each detached scout will have to work out a solution of the situation for himself.

If the patrol is suddenly attacked or surprised by a superior force, the members should at once scatter in all directions and make their way independently to the last place designated as a rendezvous or meeting place, and then after uniting continue the reconnaissance. It should be the invariable rule never to quit a reconnaissance until some result has been obtained.

When the patrol has discovered a hostile patrol and our patrol leader has little doubt that the enemy has seen his men, he should continue his forward movement, by a covered approach, if possible, in order to gain the flank or rear of the hostile patrol. He should do nothing to show the enemy that his men have been seen by him. If the patrol has to cross an open patch of ground in this case they should do so at a rapid pace and in extended order so that if the enemy open fire they will have a poor target. Having gained a covered locality the patrol will rapidly change its position to a flank, approach the enemy's patrol from an unexpected direction and endeavor to ambuscade it or in any case force it to retire. The object of great secrecy no longer exists because the enemy's patrol has seen our men and it is desirable to keep him busy in this locality and away from our own lines and prevent his sending back information.

If, despite all precautions that have been taken, the patrol falls into an ambuscade, it should attack boldly. Courage and coolness may wrest success from the most adverse circumstances.

When the patrol has discoverd a force of the enemy worth while reporting the disposition must be such as to permit the patrol leader to make his observation of the hostile force in comparative security. With this end in view he must get to a vantage point from which he may obtain a good view. The remaining members of the patrol must be so disposed as to guard all avenues of approach from the known direction of the enemy's forces in order to prevent surprise. The number of observers allowed to look out should be limited, the remaining members of the patrol being completely concealed. The lookout men must expose themselves more or less to obtain a good view and the more men that are thus employed the greater the risk of detection. It is the natural tendency of every man on dangerous service to keep a lookout for himself, but it is the duty of the patrol leader to make the necessary dispositions for observation and security and to insure that all unemployed men keep under cover and are not spending their time craning their necks to see and taking a chance on giving away his position.

In cases where the enemy has his outpost line posted along a ridge the patrol commander may be able to find a concealed position well to the flank where he is able to observe. By going there and then having the other members of the patrol advance against the front of the line and open fire making a big show of strength by a rapid fusillade he may be able to locate some of the sentinels and outguards by noting the location from which combat patrols are sent out, and from the general confusion along the entire line. The best time for such an operation is at daybreak when the outposts are being changed and there is more or less confusion along the line. The selected point should be gained before dawn.

If one of the members of the patrol is fired at by an enemy from his concealed position it is a good plan for him to drop as though hit, look around for a bit of cover, then stagger towards it and drop again. Human nature will persuade the enemy to come out and inspect their "bag" and when they move out into the open they will be an easy target for the other men of the patrol. If this ruse fails the patrol must work around the flank of the scout to see if he is really hit.

When the patrol discovers a considerable body of troops advancing towards the position of their own main body they should open fire with a perfect fusilade. This is for the purpose of not only delaying the enemy but also giving warning to our own troops in order that they may be prepared to meet the attack. There is no longer any necessity for secrecy and the more noise the patrol can make the better.

Night Operations The operations of a patrol sent out from an outpost line at night varies considerably from that by day, especially when the night is very dark or the country is close. By day the hostile scout will be found occupying the high ground. At night he will reverse his position and seek the low ground so that all persons approaching will be seen on the sky line. Any considerable body of the enemy will be confined to roads and well defined trails and if he wanders far from these operations will be so hampered that he will be able to accomplish little.

If the patrol advances right down the road or trail they will simply run into the enemy without any warning and any information obtained will be incomplete because the patrol leader will not know whether he has struck an isolated patrol, the advance point of a larger force or a patrolling post sent out from the hostile outpost line.

The patrol should use the road or trail as a line of direction merely and not march along it themselves.

If the country alongside the road is too difficult for the patrol to traverse on account of dense woods and undergrowth, swamps, precipitous ground, etc., the enemy's patrols will also be confined to the road and a plan of action must be adopted to meet the situation.   In this case the situation we would like to produce when we meet the enemy is that he should be advancing while we are halted.   It is necessary for the patrol to get forward to the place it has been ordered to go to and it cannot do this by standing still and waiting for the enemy to come along.   The most satisfactory solution appears to be that we should always have a part of our patrol advancing and part listening.   This may be accomplished by sending two men forward only 20 or 30 yards to the front and then when they report "all clear" join them with the remainder of the patrol. This operation is constantly repeated.   The same procedure may be adopted, reversed, when retiring after having gained the object of the night reconnaissance or the patrol may be ordered to disperse and make their way back as individuals so that in case of interception by the enemy there will be a probability of someone escaping with the information that has been gained.

In more open terrain the patrol will move across country twenty or thirty yards from the road in a manner similar to that described above, being careful to have scouts examine the road from time to time.

The knowledge of the country in front of the outpost by day patrolling will stand well in hand when night work has to be done.   If it be found necessary to detach a scout to reconnoiter to the front or flanks the patrol will remain halted until his return. If the patrol should follow him without waiting for his report the whole party may just as well have moved in the first place.

If the scout and the patrol are to move to a new rendezvous by different routes the difficulties of night work are simply being multiplied. It is difficult enough to find one suitable route at night and much more so to find two that will meet at a certain point. It is difficult to distinguish friend from enemy and there is great danger on this account in any dispersion of the patrol.

Both for safety and concealment at night the patrol will have to advance in a close formation. In darkness a group offers a very little better target than does an individual and accurate fire is not to be expected. In any sudden encounter at close quarters, unless against an overwhelming force, there is a tactical advantage in concentration. The patrol must conform instantly to the movements or direction of the leader.

If the patrol has to remain out over night the location of the bivouac should be selected before dusk, but should not be occupied until after dark. After selecting a suitable spot the patrol should continue its operations for a time and then as soon as it is dark make its way back to the bivouac. This is done in order to deceive any of the enemy's scouts that may have the patrol under observation.

It is generally unsafe to light fires at night; smoking and the lighting of matches by members of the patrol must be positively prohibited. The former not only gives a glow that can be seen for several hundred yards but emits an odor of tobacco that may be distinguished for a considerable distance.

Returning The methods to be employed by the patrol leader in getting his patrol back home after having accomplished his mission will depend upon the action of the enemy and the nature of the country.

If the patrol is being pursued by the enemy it will of course have to get back as best it can but there is always a question as to whether it is better to put up a fight or to avoid combat. If the patrol leader has not secured all the information that he desires it is better to try to get away without a scrap and after getting clear of the enemy and reaching cover, return by a different route and continue the reconnaissance. If you stop to engage in a combat you are losing time. If the patrol leader has obtained all the information he is after it may be well to engage the enemy's patrol so as to give warning of his approach towards the outpost line, in which case the patrol leader would keep all his men under immediate control and not allow them to scatter.

The patrol commander can never be certain that one or more of the enemy's patrols have not eluded him as he advanced and is now operating between himself and his own outpost line, so that in returning every precaution must be taken to prevent being caught between two hostile detachments.

This is also a reason why such great precautions

have to be taken in sending messengers back, as there is danger of their falling into the hands of the enemy's patrols who may have worked around the flanks and be lying in wait for them.

CHAPTER VIII

Reconnaissance of Ground

The scout must know where to look and what to look for. He must be able to estimate the military value of natural and artificial features of the country and of what he sees of the enemy. He must be able to embody the results of his observations in a concise report either orally or in writing which will enable his superior to form a clear idea of the subject and grasp it in all its details as if he himself had made the reconnaissance.

You should get clearly into your mind the elements to be considered in making a reconnaissance of the various features that you may be called upon to examine. Thus if you are sent out to make an examination of a bridge you will know at once what to look for and how to look for it. These elements are herein arranged in groups which make them convenient for study. Do not neglect them. They may prove most useful some day.

General: Local name of road.
Roads   General direction. Names of
important places connected, and their distance apart. State condition of repair Note position, distance and appearance of any prominent landmarks and accurately describe them so that they may be easily identified and useful to troops marching on road. Note any places that would require repairs before road could be used by artillery and trains. Note location and state general characteristics of country in vicinity.

75

Width: State width in feet. Note any material alteration in width. Contraction might check column or necessitate decrease in front. Expansion may permit increase in front of column or afford halting places. Nine feet required for infantry in column of squads and cavalry in column of twos; 16 feet are necessary to permit wagons to pass.

Construction: Macadam, corduroy, plank or dirt. Note available materials for repair, such as stone quarries for resurfacing or woods suitable for corduroying. Note any places that are liable to be badly cut up and rutted in wet weather with heavy or continuous traffic.

Grades: Make note of any grades that would affect rate of march of troops or trains. Estimate grade and state distance covered.

Borders: Whether woods, hedges, fences or ditches. Nature of woods, dense, open or underbrush. Class and height of hedges and fences and whether or not they screen road. Nature of ditches and whether they form an obstacle to deployment and the possibility of their use in case of attack against flank of column.

Surrounding Country: Nature of—open fields, woods, hedges, fences, level or broken up by ravines, defiles, embankments, heights that command, rivers, swamps and small streams. Any features that would give natural cover for or affect deployment and advance of the enemy or your own troops.

Lateral Roads: Points where they leave the main road. Places to which they lead. Construction and width. Any general information obtainable.

Parallel Roads: Places which they connect. Distance from main road. Construction and width. Any general information which may be obtainable.

Railroads *General:* Local name. Principal places connected within theatre of operations. Junction points, name of and places to which diverging line runs. Kind of fuel used. Grades that affect transportation. Proximity of roads parallel to line. Character or borders of right of way, wire fences, etc. General nature of country through which railroad passes.

The Line: Single or double track. Gauge. Ballast. Weight of rails. Class of ties. Signal system. Location of water tanks. Tunnels. Cuttings. Embankments. Sharp curves. Sidings other than at stations.

Bridges and Trestles: Location. Class and construction. Length. Height above water. Abutments and piers. Materials available for repair in case of disablement or destruction.

Stations: Name. Defensibility. Platforms, length, width, height, material. Loading ramps, or material in vicinity for construction of. Yards, number of tracks with total car capacity or length in feet. Shelter for troops. Buildings available for hospitals and storehouses. Open spaces for forming troops and storing supplies. Facilities for unloading and loading troops and supplies. Lighting arrangements.

Communications: Number of telegraph wires, class of supports. General construction. Telephone system. Materials for repairs.

Rolling Stock: Number of different classes of cars available. Capacity of each class. Number of engines.

Shops: Location. Capacity. Turntables. Round houses. Inspection pits. Spare parts and stores available. Material for construction and repair work.

Rivers   *General:* Local name. General direction of flow. Piers or landing stages available or material for constructing them. Note roads leading towards or parallel to. Places where dams could be made to inundate valley.

Width: Stated in feet. Does it vary much in different places.

Depth: Is it navigable throughout the theatre of operations. If not state what the obstructions to navigation are. If navigable state for what kind of boats. If tidal give range of tide. Is it liable to floods. Note range of floods by debris on shore or mud on trees. Does it dry up in summer.

Current: Velocity in miles per hour. To determine this pace off 100 yards on the bank. Weight a stick at one end and throw it into the stream so that one end sticks out of the water. Note the time that it takes to float the 100 yards. If it floats the distance in 100 seconds the stream is flowing 2 miles per hour; 80 seconds 2½ miles per hour; 70 seconds 3 miles; 60 seconds 3½ miles;

50 seconds, 4 miles; 45 seconds, 4½ miles; 40 seconds,
5 miles; 35 seconds, 6½ miles; 30 seconds, 7 miles;
25 seconds, 8 miles; 20 seconds, 10 miles.

Banks: Character — steep, sloping gradually,
wooded. Height of top above the water. Which
bank commands approaches. Banks of streams
are designated right and left as they are on the right
or left of the observer facing in the direction of the
flow.

Islands: Location. Extent. Wooded or sand
bars. Available for passage or constructing bridges.

Fords: Depth: Safe depths; cavalry 4 ft.; infantry
3 ft.; artillery 2 ft. 4 in.; wagons 3 ft. In sluggish
stream add 25% for cavalry and infantry. Is it
always passable? In tidal stream or one subject
to freshets it may become impassable in a few hours.

Width: Note direction by reference to easily
distinguishable features on banks.

Bottom: Sand, mud, gravel, rock. The two
latter are best. Mud and sand bottom rapidly
increase in depth when troops and animals ford it.
Large stones are bad for cavalry and wheeled
vehicles.

Approaches: Character on both sides especially for
wheeled vehicles. Are banks steep or gradual.
Would it be necessary to cut ramps. If banks
are low and soft is there brushwood and trees at
hand for corduroying.

Fords may be found by looking for tracks or
paths on banks. They are often oblique, especially
where river makes a double bend, and run from
salient to salient through the silting up of the new
bank.

Facilities for Crossing: Selection of site. Point chosen must be close to road to facilitate bringing up material and troops. Islands reduce length but water may be deep on one side. Banks, will ramps be required. Nature of country on far side, favorable for deployment and defense. Materials available: timber, rope, wire, railway ties, rails, spikes, bolts, etc. Cover for defenders. Note positions that command location that could be occupied by the enemy.

Ferries: Locality, approaches, landing places, capacity and number of boats, methods of propulsion. Can guns be crossed, can animals be walked across or will they have to swim. Time taken to cross. Materials for constructing rafts.

Bridges   *Class:* King post, Queenpost, truss, suspension, etc.

Construction: Material, wood, iron, stone, concrete. Number of bays or spans. How supported and thickness of supports.

Roadway: Width and general characteristics.

Approaches: Character on both sides. Any feature that would delay progress of troops or trains. Facilities for deployment after crossing.

General: Height above water. Depth of water. Length in feet. Fords in vicinity. Safe for all arms and trains. Materials available for repairs. How could passage be effected if bridge was destroyed. How could bridge be most easily destroyed or rendered impassable. Is bridge commanded by high ground on far side or to the flanks.

Towns and Villages

General: Local name. Area covered. Population; allow about 5 persons per house. General occupation of inhabitants. Note shops and materials useful to military. Telephone and telegraph connections. Prominent salients.

Position: With respect to road or other natural feature. Is it in a valley, on a plain or on hills. Is it commanded by hills.

Buildings: Approximate number. Material of which constructed. Class. Nature of roofs, flat, peaked, thatch, tile, galvanized iron. Any available for hospitals. Quarters for troops.

Defensibility: Strongest and weakest sides. Field of fire. Clearing required. Lookout points. Garrison required to defend. Cover for first line and reserves. Materials and tools for preparation for defense. Water supply. Buildings near perimeter.

Occupied by Enemy: Points from which it may be shelled by artillery. Extent of clearings in front of defenses. Obstacles. Strength of garrison. Nature of defenses. Is it supported by other positions? Position from which it could be enfiladed. Ground that commands. Possible lines of advance with advantages and disadvantages. Salients. Cover for attacking troops. Sketch showing these points would be most desirable.

Buildings

General: Location, detached or otherwise. Approximate space covered. Shape. Height. Material. Thickness of walls. Roof, flat or sloping.

Material. Field of fire. Doors and windows, size, where located with respect to field of fire. Outbuildings, removable. Water supply. Materials for preparation for defense, making barricades and obstacles. Cellar or basement. Practicability of making loop holes. Any ground in vicinity that commands. Any covered approaches or dead spaces that enemy could use. Latrines.

Woods   *Extent:* Approximate area covered. Detached or part of general forest.

Nature: Close or open.

Trees: Nature, height. Deciduous trees shed leaves in the fall and furnish less cover during winter months than in summer when they are in full leaf.

Undergrowth: Height and density. How far can you see through?

Roads and Trails: Nature of. Where they lead. Could guns move off road.

Clearings: Location and extent.

Hills   *Location:* Isolated or a part of range.

Height: Approximate height above surrounding country. Note steepness that would impede movement of troops.

Surface: Wooded, rocky, grassland, deep ravines, convex or concave.

Command: Extent of view. Important points commanded with artillery or rifle fire. Ranges to same. Signal stations available.

Roads and Trails: Nature of. Where they lead to. Note steep grades that would impede progress of troops and trains.

Defiles   *Nature:* Straight or winding. Direction. Length, breadth and open spaces. Width, frontage of column that could pass through. Character of country on flanks, accessible or inaccessible. Approaches, commanded by heights. Exit, commanded by high ground to front. Spaces available for deployment on debouching.

General: Practicability as line of advance for troops of all arms. If strong points held by enemy, how could he be turned out? Can advance be blocked by obstacles? Can exit be covered by friendly troops?

Having taken the necessary steps to get into touch with the enemy's main forces the scout or patrol will endeavor to find out the details of his strength, composition and probable intentions.

Reconnaissance of the Enemy   In reporting upon the enemy in bivouac the following points will be covered:

1. General location of bivouac.
2. Strength.
3. Composition.
4. Outposts. Strength and composition. General line of supports. Line of observation. Patrols sent out. Detached posts. Does he appear to be on the alert? Approaches. Obstacles.

In reporting upon the enemy occupying a defensive position as many of the following points as practicable will be included in the report:

1. General location of position. Direction and extent of front covered.
2. Strength and composition of troops on the line.
3. Field fortifications, class and location.
4. Where do flanks rest.
5. Location of reserves.
6. Location of artillery.
7. Nature of approaches to position. Cover for attacking troops. Position for guns.
8. Approaches for flank attack. Possibility of turning movement.
9. Obstacles, natural and artificial.
10. Position, strength and composition of outposts. Do they appear to be vigilant.
11. System of patroling to front and flanks.

In reporting the movements of the enemy on the march the following points should be included:

1. General direction of march.
2. Strength and composition.
3. System of covering detachments. Strength of advance guard. Independent cavalry. Flank guards. Rear guards.
4. Formation of column.
5. Location of trains—are they adequately protected.
6. Any straggling.

CHAPTER IX

Messages .

The information gained by patrols is sent back by messengers in the form of either a oral or written message. The patrol leader should be provided with a book of army field message blanks that are issued to the service by the Signal Corps.

The heading must be carefully filled in as follows:

From: Here inset name of sending detachment, for example: Corporal Allen's Patrol or Patrol No. 1—Support No. 2, or such designation as will surely identify the patrol.

At: Enter the location of the patrol at the time the message is sent in. This serves to eliminate the necessity of repetition in the body of the message. It is important that your commanding officer know just exactly where you were when you wrote the message for it will be of great assistance, when he reads your message and compares the localities mentioned with his maps. For example: 200 yards south of cross roads 47. Edge of woods 400 yards west of Hanly house. Hill ½ mile east of observatory.

Date: Always date a message, placing the day of the month first, following this with the month and year, for example: 12-May-15.

Hour: The exact hour of signing the message should be entered here. This is important on account of the possibility of other messages coming

U. S. ARMY FIELD MESSAGE	No.	Sent by	Time	Rec'd by	Time	Check
Communicated by BUZZER, PHONE TELEGRAPH, WIRELESS, LANTERN, HELIO, FLAG, CYCLIST, FOOT MESSENGER, MOUNTED MESSENGER. (Underscore means used)		This	Space for	Signal Operator	rs Only.	

From _____ NAME OF SENDING DETACHMENT HERE

At _____ LOCATION OF SENDING DETACHMENT HERE

Date _____ Hour _____ No. _____

To _____

_____

_____

_____

_____

_____

_____

_____

_____

_____

_____

Received _____

_____

in and the time each was written may be determining factors in making an estimate of the situation.

Number: Messages should be numbered serially
by each patrol each time they go out. This is
necessary in order that your officer may know
whether or not he has received all the messages
that you have sent in. Say he receives your
message No. 1 and an hour later receives No. 3,
he knows at once that No. 2 is missing and can take
the necessary action in the matter.

The method of sending messages should be
understood.

The body of the message should convey to your
officer the information that you desire to report,
and the following points should be observed.

(*a*) Stick to the points you have been ordered to
report upon.

(*b*) Word it just as you would a telegram, but
don't leave out any essentials.

(*c*) Write clearly. Your message may have to
be read by the flickering light of a match or the
glow from a cigar. Proper names should be written
in block letters so there can be no mistake.

(*d*) Report only facts that you have been able to
personally verify. If you give second hand information or deductions state from where it came or
on what your deductions are based.

(*e*) In reporting on the enemy try to cover the
following points: By whom seen. How many.
What arms. Where. What doing.

(*f*) Your message should end up with a statement
of what you intend to do. For example, I remain

here in observation.   I will go to Allen's Ranch.
Will return to hill 43.   Will fall back along hill road,
etc.   This is desirable so that your officers may
know what you are going to do or where to find you
in case of necessity.

Trifling details have no place in a military message.   Your officer wants to know about the things
he has sent you out to find.   Usually he wants to
know whether or not the enemy is or has been at a
certain place, his composition, numbers and his
system of covering detachments.   If he has not been
there it is also important to know this so that a
negative report would not be out of place.   He does
not want descriptions of your encounters with hostile
scouts and narratives of your adventures.

A little information gotten back promptly is
worth volumes of writing sent in too late.

If there is any possibility of the messenger being
intercepted by the enemy the message should be
sent in by two routes each bearer taking a different
one.   The messenger should know the contents of
his message so that in case he has to destroy it and
finally makes his getaway he can make a verbal
report of the contents.

Verbal messages are not used except when there
is no time to prepare a written one.   This is on
account of the liability of the messenger getting
information mixed up into an unintelligible statement.   At maneuvers I have seen a mounted man
come riding down the road with a supposed message,
and by the time he reached the officer to whom he

was to report, he had either forgotten or had never been told what to report.

Practice in message writing is one of the subjects to be included in the scout's education and he should be given a thorough course of training in it.

CHAPTER X

Signals and Signaling

Communication between members of a patrol is maintained by means of visual signals so that the scout must be an expert in this line of work. He must be familiar with the arm signals and he must be able to send and receive messages in both the wigwag and semaphore codes.

Arm Signals The following arm signals adapted for the use of scouts are laid down in the Drill Regulations and when signaled from the patrol leader to detached scouts they indicate the following:

Forward March: Carry the hand to the shoulder, straighten and hold the arm horizontally, thrusting it in the direction of the march. To indicate to the detached scout that he is to move forward.

Halt: Carry the hand to the shoulder, thrust the hand upward and hold the arm vertically. To halt and take cover.

Double Time, March: Carry the hand to the shoulder, rapidly thrust the hand upward several times to the full extent of the arm. To continue in the direction signaled at a rapid gait.

Squads Right, March: Raise the arm laterally until horizontal, carry it to a vertical position above the head and swing it several times between the vertical and horizontal positions. To move by the right flank until you get the signal for forward march or to the rear march.

90

Squads Left, March: Raise the arm laterally until horizontal, carry it downward to the side and swing it several times between the downward and horizontal positions. To move by the left flank until you get the signal for forward march or to the rear march.

To the Rear, March: Extend the arm vertically above the head, carry it laterally downward to the side and swing it several times between the vertical and downward positions. To move to the rear until you get the signal to halt.

Assemble: Raise the arm vertically to its full extent and describe horizontal circles. To move towards the patrol leader.

In addition to the above signals the Field Service Regulations authorize the following:

Enemy in Sight in Small Numbers: Hold the rifle above the head horizontally.

Enemy in Sight in Force: Same as preceding, raising and lowering the rifle several times.

Have Important Information: Extend both arms laterally to full extent. Signaled from a detached scout, the patrol commander will either join the scout to observe for himself or will send one of his spare men to relieve the scout in order that he may come in and make an oral report.

Visual Signaling

For the wigwag flag used with the General Service Code, there is one position and there are three motions. The position is with the flag held vertically, the signalman facing directly towards the station with which it is desired to communicate. The first motion (the dot) is to

the right of the sender and will embrace an arc of
90 degrees, starting with the vertical position and
returning to it, and will be made in a plane at right
angles to the line connecting the two stations. The
second motion (the dash) is a similar motion to the
left of the sender. The third motion (front) is
downward directly in front of the sender and
instantly returned to the vertical position. This is
used to indicate a pause or conclusion.

The following is the *International* or *General Service Code*.

Alphabet

A . —   N — .
B — . . .   O — — —
C — . — .   P . — — .
D — . .   Q — — . —
E .   R . — .
F . . — .   S . . .
G — — .   T —
H . . . .   U . . —
I . .   V . . . —
J . — — —   W . — —
K — . —   X — . . —
L . — . .   Y — . — —
M — —   Z — — . .

Numerals

1 . — — — —   6 — . . . .
2 . . — — —   7 — — . . .
3 . . . — —   8 — — — . .
4 . . . . —   9 — — — — .
5 . . . . .   0 — — — — —

Punctuation

Period...................................`· · · · · · ·`
Comma.................................`· — · — · —`
Interrogation...........................`· · — — · ·`

To call a station, make its call letter until acknowledged, at intervals giving the call or signal of the calling station. If the call letter of a station is unknown, signal A(· —) at intervals followed by the call or signal of the calling station until acknowledged.

To acknowledge a call, signal **MM** (— — — —), **front,** followed by the call letter of the acknowledging station.

If the sender discovers that he has made an error, he should make **AA** (· — · —), **front,** after which he begins the word in which the error occurred.

To break or stop signals from the sending station, make the signal **BK**(— · · · — · —), **front.**

To start the sending station again, signal **CC, front, A, front** (— · — · — · — ·, **front,** · —, **front**), followed by the last word correctly received. The sender will then resume his message, beginning with the word indicated by the receiver.

Each word, abbreviation, or conventional signal is followed by a **front.**

Conventional Visual Signals

End of a word........**front.**
End of sentence......**front, front.**
End of message.......**front, front, front.**
Signature follows.....**s i g, front.**

Error...............A A, front.
Acknowledgment ....M M, front.
Cease signaling.......M M M, front.
Repeat after (word)...C C, front, A, front (word).
Repeat last word.....C C, front, front.
Repeat last message...C C C, front, front, front.
Move a little to right..R R, front.
Move a little to left...L L, front.
Move up hill.........U U, front.
Move down hill......D D, front.
Signal faster........F F, front.
Wait a moment...... • — • • •, front.
To break or stop send-
    ing................B K, front.

Signaling by Hand Flags with the Two-Arm Semaphore Code Hand flags are authorized for general use by the Army, though on account of their short range they are of limited application and are chiefly serviceable for use in communication between members of a patrol and for incidental signaling.

The range, with flags of the usual size is dependent upon light and background, but is seldom more than one mile with the naked eye. It is limited to visual signaling work. It will be found useful under many circumstances and is adapted to special work when rapid communication for short distances is needed.

Hand flags are used in the same manner as the semaphore machine except that in making the interval the flags are crossed downward in front of the body (just above the knees).

The end of a message is two successive "chop-chop" signals and withdrawing the flags from view. To make the "chop-chop" signal both arms are placed at the right horizontal and then moved up and down in a cutting motion.

In calling a station face it squarely and make its call. If there is no immediate reply wave the flags over the head to attract attention, making the call at frequent intervals.

When the sender makes "end of message," the receiver, if message is understood, extends the flags horizontally and waves them until the sender does the same, when both may leave their stations.

Great care must be taken with hand flags to hold the staffs so as to form a prolongation of the arms.

The scout should practice signaling with the arms alone for he may be in such a position that he will not be able to use a flag and at times have no flag to use.

Conventional Signals   To call or answer: "Attention," followed by the call letter of the station called. Repeat as necessary.

Both signalmen then make "Interval."

Repeat last word: C C, interval, interval.

Repeat last message: C C C, interval, interval, interval.

Repeat after (word): C C interval, A (word).

End of word: Interval.

End of sentence: Chop signal.

TWO-ARM SEMIPHORE CODE.

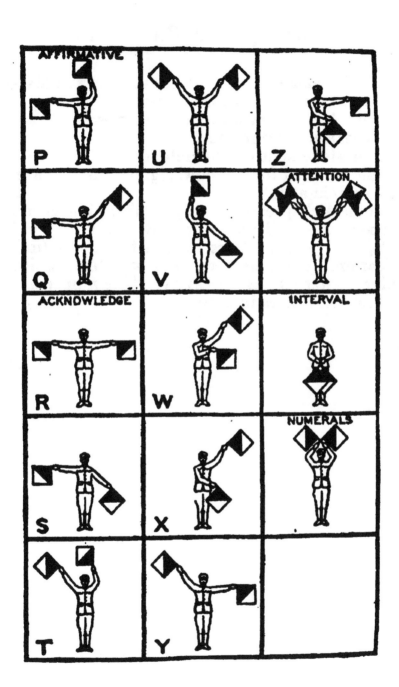

End of Message: Two successive chop signals and then withdraw the flags from view.

Error: A A Interval then repeat word.

To break in: Attention.

Acknowledgment or understood: R.

While waiting for acknowledgment, or in case of delay remain at interval.

"Numerals" precedes every combination of numbers sent and indicates numerals until interval is made, after which letters recur without any further indication. When numerals follow letters no intervening "interval" is necessary. The numerals are the first ten letters in order.

CHAPTER XI

Map Reading

In order to make use of maps that may be furnished or may come into his possession, the scout must have some knowledge of map reading to the extent indicated as follows:

1. A knowledge of scales so that he will have an understanding of the relation between the distances shown on the map and the actual distances on the ground.

2. A knowledge of the conventional signs that are used in map making to illustrate the natural and artificial features of the country covered by the map.

3. A knowledge of direction in order that he will be able to orient his map and find his position on it and will be able in writing his reports to accurately describe the direction of one point from another.

4. An elementary knowledge of the methods used by sketchers in showing the difference of elevation on military maps.

A military map is one which shows the relative distances, elevations and directions of all objects of military importance in the area represented and by map reading is meant the ability to grasp not only the general features of the map but to form a mental picture of the appearance of the ground represented. This means the ability to convert map distances into corresponding ground distances; to get a clear idea of the net work of streams, roads, woods and other natural and artificial features of the country; to grasp quickly the relative direction of points from each other and to form a clear conception of heights, slopes, lowlands and other features represented.

It is not the intention to lay down in this little book a complete treatise on the subject of map reading, you can get that from one of several good text books on the subject. You will find it an interesting subject and the more expert you become in it the more value you will be as a scout.

Scales   All maps are drawn to scale, that is each unit of distance on the map must bear a fixed proportion to the corresponding distance on the ground. If the scale of the map is three inches to one mile any three inches on the map will represent one mile on the ground, an inch and a half on the map will represent a half mile on the ground.

On all military maps you will find the scale on which the map was drawn. Our regulations provide that they shall be three inches to one mile for road sketches and 6 inches to 1 mile for position sketches This scale may be shown or expressed in one of three ways:

1. By a plain statement in words and figures of this relation of the map distance to the ground distance, for example 3 inches to 1 mile.

2. By a representative fraction in which the numerator represents the map distance and the denominator represents the ground distance, thus 1:21,120 would be the R. F. for 3 inches to 1 mile,

that is any one unit of measure on the map would represent 21,120 of those same units on the ground. The R. F. for 6 inches would be 1:10,560.

3. By a graphical scale in which a line is drawn on the map and divided into equal parts each part being marked, not with its actual length, but with the distance which it represents on the ground.

The scales usually employed are inserted herein for your use. There is no necessity for your burdening your mind with a lot of complicated mathematical problems on the solution of scales.

The usual scale on the map will be shown in yards as a unit of measure. The scale that you will use in determining distances on the ground will be in paces. The distance that an ordinary man covers with each step is from 30 to 36 inches. The scales shown range between these length paces for 3 inches to 1 mile and 6 inches to 1 mile. They should be all you will have use for.

You must know the length of your pace. This may be determined by going to the target range and pacing from the targets to the 500 yard firing point. This is 18,000 inches. Divide this figure by the number of paces you took in covering the distance. This will be the number of inches in your pace. Now pace from the 200 yard to the 600 yard firing point. This is 400 yards or 14,400 inches. Likewise divide the number of paces that you took into 14,400 and it will give you the number of inches in your pace between these two points. Now pace back to the 300 yard firing point and determine the length of your pace for the course. To get your average add the three together and divide by three and take the nearest number of even inches as the length of your pace. This will be sufficiently accurate for all practical purposes.

To measure distances on the map simply apply the graphical scale to the points between which you

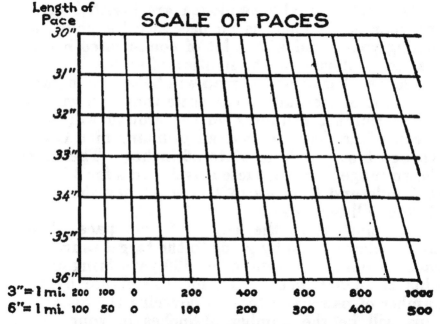

desire to measure and read the distance direct. To measure the distance along a winding road use a slip of paper and a pencil. By placing the point of the pencil on the edge of the slip of paper at each successive point where the direction changes the paper may be twisted around and made to follow the bends of the road until the total distance has been covered, when a mark should be made on the paper. Apply the edge of the paper to the scale on the map and determine the total distance. Don't waste time figuring this out. Go to one of your officers and he can show you in a minute how to do it and then a little practice will make you proficient.

Conventional Signs In the drawing of a military map the maker uses certain conventional signs to represent the military features of cover, obstacles, communication, etc., and with these you should be familiar. It will be seen that an effort has been made in showing these features to imitate the general appearance of the objects as seen from a point directly overhead so that you will rarely have any trouble in recognizing the meaning of a symbol that you have never seen before. There is a constant tendency towards simplicity and very often only the outline of the object, such as woods, cultivated ground, etc., is indicated with the growth written inside the outline. This latter method is the rule rather than the exception in hasty military sketching. All open spaces on military maps are grass land.

Direction The four cardinal points of the compass are north, east, south and west. The compass circle is graduated in degrees from zero in a direction following the movement of the hands of a clock to 360. Thus when the compass is oriented the 0-360 degree mark points north, the 90 degree mark is to

Railroads

Single Track	┼┼┼┼┼┼┼┼┼┼┼┼┼┼┼┼
Double Track	▦▦▦▦▦▦▦▦▦▦▦
Electric	▭▭▭▭▭▭▭▭

Roads

Improved	═══════════
Unimproved	┄┄┄┄┄┄┄┄┄┄
Trail	┅ ┅ ┅ ┅ ┅ ┅ ┅

Cemetery

Church	
Post Office	
Waterworks	

Fences

Hedge	
Stone	
Worm	∿∿∿∿∿∿∿∿
Wire, barbed	–x–––x–––x–––x–––x–
Wire, smooth	–o–––o–––o–––o–––o–

Trees

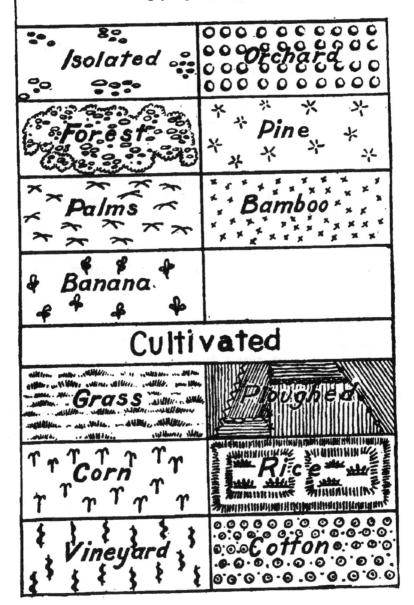

Isolated

Orchard

Forest

Pine

Palms

Bamboo

Banana

Cultivated

Grass

Ploughed

Corn

Rice

Vineyard

Cotton

the east, the 180 degree mark is to the south and the 270 degree mark is to the west. You should use these points of the compass in reports whenever you have to refer to direction.

In order that directions on the map and ground shall coincide it is necessary that the map be oriented, that is, placed in such position that every road, stream or other feature on the map will be parallel to its actual position on the ground. This enables you to pick out and identify on the ground all features shown on the map.

The map may be oriented by any of the following methods:

1. When the map has a magnetic meridian on it. Place the north and south line of the compass on the magnetic meridian and turn the map until the north end of the needle points to the north of the circle. If the magnetic meridian is not shown on the map you must know the declination of the needle and place one on it. If the declination is not more than 4 or 5 degrees the orientation on the true meridian or along the up and down borders of the map will be sufficiently accurate for all practical purposes.

2. When you have no compass or the meridian is not shown on the map—(a) If you can locate on the map your position on the ground and can identify another place on the map which you can see on the ground, shift the map around until the two points on the map are aligned on the distant point on the ground and you have the map oriented. (b) By reference to a straight road or line of railway

on which you may be standing turn the map until the conventional symbol on the map points in the same direction as the feature it represents.

In both of these methods the points used for orientation should be as far apart as possible and in any case they should be more than an inch apart on the map.

To find your position on a map—(a) When the map has been oriented by compass, sight a ruler at an object on the ground and while keeping the ruler on the plotted position of this object on the map draw a line towards yourself. Repeat this operation with respect to a second point located at an angle as nearly a right angle as possible. The intersection of these two lines is your map position. Check it up with the features in your immediate vicinity.

(b) When your map has been oriented on two points sight your ruler at some point as nearly at right angles to your orienting line as possible and keeping it on the plotted point on the map draw a line towards you that cuts the orienting line. At the point of this intersection is your map position.

You will ordinarily be able to locate yourself on the map with sufficient accuracy for all practical purposes by examining the ground and comparing it with the map.

When you have no compass for orienting your map you may find the approximate true north by the following method when the sun is shining: Point the hour hand of your watch towards the sun. A line drawn from the pivot center of the dial mid-

way between the outer end of the hour hand and
12 o'clock will point south and a prolongation of
this line in the opposite direction will point north.
Having determined a north and south line on the
ground by noting two physical objects orient your
map on these.   Fig. 1.

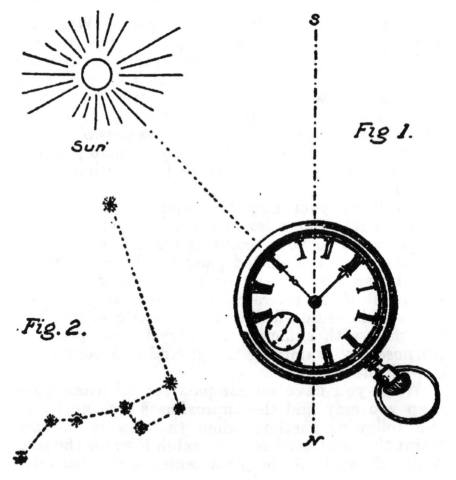

Sun

Fig 1.

Fig. 2.

At night you will be able to determine the approximate true north by facing the North star, which lies nearly in prolongation of a line of the two outer stars of the bowl of the great dipper, Fig. 2.

Contours Only an elementary knowledge of contours is necessary for you. Do not waste your time working out mathematical problems relating to horizontal equivalents, map distances, vertical intervals and slopes. These are all very nice if you have time to go thoroughly into the subject of military topography but they have no place here. A contour is a line drawn around a hill having the same level throughout its length. Its object is to show the actual and comparative heights, the shape and slopes of the ground.

All contours join or extend to the edge of the map. When they join they either represent a hill top or a depression. A hill when the smallest closed contour is higher than the adjoining one and a depression when it is lower. Where the slope is uniform the contours are equally spaced, when it is gradual they are wide apart and when it is steep they are close together.

A water shed is the high ground between two valleys. The water flows away from it on both sides and is indicated by the higher contours bulging out towards the lower ones.

A water-course is the low ground between two watersheds, the rain from both sides of it joins in one stream and is indicated by the contours bending sharply towards the higher ones.

When contours of different elevation join togeth
and form one line they indicate a cliff.   Where
higher one crosses a lower one it is an overhangi
cliff.

A saddle or col is the space between the summi
of two adjacent hills.   It is indicated by two co
tours of greater elevation on two opposite sides
it and two contours of less elevation on the oth
sides.

There are other methods of showing topograph
features on a map, namely by shading hachurin
which is merely shading by a series of parallel p
strokes.   In both instances the tops of hills are l
white while the hill sides are covered with shadi
which is made darkest where the slopes are steepe

There is no easy road to success in map readin
You will have to work to acquire the accomplis
ment.   Get the contents of this chapter firm
fixed in your mind, then get a map of the surroundi
country and go out on the ground and study a
compare the one with the other.   Practice orienti
your map and learn practically the problems of t
visibility of one point from another.

CHAPTER XII
First Aid

When the necessity arises for the employment of first Aid you will probably be out by yourself or one of a small patrol far from a place where medical attention can be secured and your knowledge of the subject may be the means of saving your own life or the life of a fellow scout.

It is not essential that you know many things to be helpful in an emergency but you must understand a few methods and know how to apply them and in ordinary cases what you can do may often be all that is necessary.

The disabling accidents that are likely to befall one or more of a party of scouts will be gun-shot wounds, less frequently shrapnel or shell wounds and saber and bayonet cuts; drowning, snake bite, and freezing and frostbite and sunstroke. It is with these that you should know how to deal if the occasion requires.

Wounds When a bullet goes through the muscles or soft parts of the body alone, generally nothing need be done except to protect the wound or wounds with the contents of the first aid packet which you should always carry on your belt.

Here are a few general rules regarding wounds that you ought to get firmly fixed in your mind:

1. Act quickly and quietly. Make the patient sit or lie down and expose the wound by cutting

away such clothing as may interfere with a careful dressing of it but do not remove more than is necessary. Burn your knife blade in the flame of several matches and pick out any bits of dirty clothing or other foreign substance that may have lodged in the wound.

2. Do not touch the wound with your fingers and do not allow any other person to touch it. Keep everybody away from the patient not actually needed to help him.

3. Above all do not put any water on the wound for all the germs of the skin in the vicinity may be washed into it, where they set up in business right away.

4. If blood is coming from the wound profusely you must take measures to stop it right away, for it is probable that either an artery or a vein has been severed and your comrade will bleed to death in a very short time. If there is just a little bleeding it is probable that the first aid compresses will stop it.

5. When bones are fractured, in addition to dressing the wound you will have to take measures to protect the flesh from the jagged ends.

6. With wounds about the body, the chest and the abdomen you must not meddle, except to protect them, when possible without much handling, with the contents of the first aid packet.

First Aid Packet To apply the contents of the first aid packet proceed as follows:

1. If there is one wound carefully remove the paper from one of the two

packages without unfolding compress or bandage and hold by grasping the outside folds between the thumb and fingers.

When ready to dress wound, open compress by pulling on the two side folds of bandage, being careful not to touch the inside of the compress with the fingers or anything else.

Still holding one roll of the bandage in each hand, apply the compress to the wound and wrap the ends of the bandage around the limb or -part near the ends, when the ends may be tied together or fastened with safety pins. The second compress and bandage may be applied over the first or may, if the arm is wounded, be used as a sling.

2. If there are two wounds opposite each other, use one compress opened out—but with the folded bandage on the back—for one wound, and hold it in place by the bandage of the compress used to cover the other wound.

3. If there are two wounds, not opposite each other, apply a compress to each.

4. If the wound is too large to be covered by the compress, find and break the stitch holding the compress together, unfold it, and apply as directed above.

Generally this is all that is necessary for the first treatment, and sometimes it is all that is needed for several days. The importance of the care with which this first dressing is made cannot be too seriously insisted upon. It is better to leave a wound undressed than to dress it carelessly or gnorantly, so that the dressing must soon be ·emoved.

Stopping Bleeding Now and then a wound will bleed very freely because a large blood vessel has been cut and you must know how to stop it. If the blood is a bright red and comes from the wound in spurts an artery has been cut. If the blood is a darker red and flows sluggishly a vein has been severed.

When bleeding is severe your patient may lose consciousness. This is due to the weak heart action so that a sufficient supply of blood does not reach the brain. To remedy this simply lower the patient's head and give your whole attention to stopping the bleeding. He will come around all right by the time you have done that.

If the bleeding be due to a ruptured artery you should endeavor to stop it by applying pressure to the artery at some point between the wound and the heart. If the bleeding be from a vein the pressure is applied directly over the wound with a tight compress or at a point between the wound and the end of the limb in which it is located. In both cases you will be able to stop the bleeding ordinarily by pressing the artery or vein against one of the bones.

When however the bleeding persists after having used these simpler methods it will usually be necessary to use a "tourniquet" and you will generally have to improvise one out of the material at hand. The compress of your first aid bandage reinforced by a rock or small chip of wood will do very well and serve to interrupt the flow of blood. After placing the compress in such position that it will press the artery against a bone the bandage may be loosely tied around the limb and any degree of pressure exerted by passing a stick under it and turning it around until the slack is taken up.

You will have to take certain precautions in the use of the tourniquet to prevent serious harm to your patient. Turn the stick very slowly and as soon as bleeding ceases stop, do not put on any more pressure. Do not use so much force that you bruise the flesh and muscles under the "tourniquet." Do not strangle the limb by keeping up the pressure too long at a time. It is a good rule to ease up on the pressure at the end of half an hour and if the bleeding does not start again leave it loose but in place ready to be used again in case of emergency.

Broken Bones   When bones are broken and splintered the idea is to get the limb in which they are located into such a position as will prevent, as far as possible any motion of the broken bone and so limit the injury to the neighboring muscles, and to lessen the pain. Straighten the limb gently by pulling on the end of it firmly and then bind splints to it with the bandage ends of your first aid packets. You will usually have to improvise splints out of any piece of wood that may be handy or from the limb of a tree. It should be padded on the side next to the limb even if you have to take your shirt to do this. The bandages should never be placed immediately over the fracture, but always above and below it. If no splint material is available the fractured arm may be bound securely to the body or the fractured leg may be bound to the sound one. Always handle a broken limb gently and do not turn or twist it any more than is absolutely necessary. Get your patient as comfortable as possible.

Drowning   One of the dangers incident to scouting is drowning. You should be able to swim, but there are times when even the best swimmer may not be able to keep himself afloat on account of some accidental injury, cramps, etc. Your knowledge of the method used to resuscitate a person who has drowned may be the means of saving the life of a comrade. The Schaefer method is here given in all its details taken bodily from the Soldiers Hand Book. Now don't merely read this over and pass it by. Here is something that you have always intended to do but never got to it. Study this method out for yourself and then get one of the men of your squad to take off his shirt and lay down on the floor and let you get the position of the operator over him, locate his lowest rib and practice the process on him a few times. Then you will know what to do and how to do it in case of accident.

Being under water for four or five minutes is generally fatal, but an effort to revive the apparently drowned should always be made unless it is known that the body has been under water for a very long time. The attempt to revive the patient should not be delayed for the purpose of removing his clothes. Begin the procedure as soon as he is out of the water, on the shore or in the boat. The first and most important thing is to start artificial respiration without delay.

Method of Resuscitation The Schaefer method is preferred because it can be carried out by one person without assistance, and because its procedure is not exhausting to the operator, thus permitting him, if required, to continue it for one or two hours. Where it is known that a person has been under water for but a few minutes, continue the artificial respiration for at least one and a half to two hours before considering the case hopeless. Once the patient has begun to breathe, watch carefully to see that he does not stop again. Should the breathing be very faint, or should he stop breathing, assist him again with artificial respiration. After he starts breathing do not lift him, nor permit him to stand until the breathing has become full and regular.

Draining Water from Air Passages.

As soon as the patient is removed from the water, turn him face to the ground, clasp your hands under his waist and raise the body so any water may drain out of the air passages while the head remains low. (See cut)

Schaefer Method

The patient is laid on his stomach, arms extended from his body beyond his head, face turned to one side so that the mouth and nose do not touch the ground. This position causes the tongue to fall forward of its own weight and so prevents its falling back into the air passages. Turning the head to one side prevents the face coming into contact with mud or water during the operation. This position also facilitates the removal from the mouth of foreign bodies such as tobacco, chewing gum, false teeth, etc., and favors the expulsion of mucus, blood, vomitus, serum, or any liquid that may be in the air passages. (See cut)

Position of Operator and Patient.

The operator kneels, straddles one or both of the patient's thighs, and faces his head. Locating the lowest rib, the operator, with his thumbs nearly parallel to his fingers, places his spread hands so that the little finger curls over the twelfth rib. If the hands are on the pelvic bones the object of the work is defeated; hence the bones of the pelvis are first located in order to avoid them. The hand must be free from the pelvis and resting on the lowest rib. By operating on the bare back it is easier to locate the lower ribs and avoid the pelvis. The nearer the ends of the ribs the hands are placed without sliding off, the better. The hands are thus removed from the spine, the fingers being nearly out of sight.

The fingers help some, but the chief pressure is exerted by the heels (thenar and hypothenar eminences) of the hands, with the weight coming straight from the shoulders. It is a waste of energy to bend the arms at the elbows and shove in from the sides, because the muscles of the back are stronger than the muscles of the arms.

The operator's arms are held straight, and his weight is brought from his shoulders by bringing his body and shoulders forward. This weight is gradually increased until at the end of the three seconds of vertical pressure upon the lower ribs of the patient the force is felt to be heavy enough to compress the parts; then the weight is suddenly removed; if there is danger of not returning the hands to the right position again they can remain lightly in place, but it is usually better to remove the hands entirely. If the operator is light, and the patient an overweight adult, he can utilize over 80 per cent of his weight by raising his knees from the ground, and supporting himself entirely on his toes and the heels of his hands, the latter properly placed on the ends of the floating ribs of the patient.   In this manner he can work as effectively as a heavy man.

A light feather, or a piece of absorbent cotton drawn out thin and held near the nose by someone, will indicate by its movements whether or not there is a current of air going and coming with each forced expiration and spontaneous inspiration.

The natural rate of breathing is twelve to fifteen times per minute.   The rate of operation should not exceed this; the lungs must be thoroughly emptied by three seconds of pressure, then refilling takes care of itself.   Pressure and release of pressure, one complete respiration, occupies about five seconds.   If the operator is alone he can be guided in each act by his own deep, regular respiration, or by counting, or by his watch lying by his side.   If comrades are present, he can be advised by them.

The duration of the efforts at artificial respiration should ordinarily exceed an hour; indefinitely longer if there are any evidences of returning animation, by way of breathing, speaking, or movements.   There are liable to be evidences of life within twenty-five minutes in patients who will recover from electric shock, but where there is doubt, the patient should have the benefit of the doubt.   In drowning, especially, recoveries are on record after two hours or more of unconsciousness; hence, the Schafer method, being easy of operation, is more likely to be persisted in.

When the operator is a heavy man it is necessary

to caution him not to bring force too violently upon the ribs, as one of them might be broken.

Do not attempt to give liquids of any kind to the patient while unconscious. Apply warm blankets and hot water bottles as soon as they can be obtained.

The Schaefer method of artificial respiration is also applicable in cases of electric shock, asphyxiation by gas, and of failure of respiration following concussion of the brain.

Snake Bites In snake bites the poison acts quickly. To prevent its entering the circulation, a bandage should be placed around the limb between the wound and the heart, and drawn tight enough to compress the veins. Then burn your knife blade in the flame of matches and cut the wound until it is well opened up and bleeds freely. Then get right down and suck the poison out of the wound. If you have a cut in your lips, there is danger of your absorbing some of the poison yourself, but to save the life of a comrade you will take this chance. The poison that is left may be destroyed by heating the blade of your knife red hot and burning out the wound. Care should be taken not to poison the patient with over-doses of whiskey. Do not give more than half a pint in four hours. Scouts should get a little bottle of permanganate of potash crystals and carry it with them. It is useful to place in a snake bite to help counteract the poison.

Freezing and Frost Bite   The frozen part, which looks white, or bluish white and is cold, should be very slowly raised in temperature by brisk but careful rubbing, in a cool place and never near a fire. The object is to restore the circulation of the blood and the natural warmth gradually and not too violently. Care and patience are necessary to accomplish this.

Sunstroke   Sunstroke or heat stroke occurs in persons exposed to high temperature either in or out of the sun. The face is flushed, skin hot and dry, breathing labored, pulse rapid and heat of body great. The patient may be unconscious. Place him in the shade. Remove his outer clothing. Wet the undershirt and try to lessen the heat of the body by cold applications to the head and surface generally. Give water as soon as he is able to swallow.